Wolfdog

By Mike O'Neill

Wolfdog

A Small Town, A Big Dog and the Family He Raised

By Mike O'Neill

Published by lulu.com 2018

ISBN: 978-0-244-71796-4

Dedication

The author thanks his remaining two brothers and two sisters for their memories of Archie, which contributed to this story. The names of many ancillary characters and the dialogue attributed to them are fictitious. The traits of Archie and the deeds he performed are true.

I thank my Ambler Writer's Group Colleagues, Karen, Kevin, Floyd and Dan for their always constructive suggestions to show, don't tell this story. It is enriched because of them.

And I thank my protagonist, Archie, for saving my life and enabling me to share his journey with you. I will never be convinced a human was not trapped inside the body of the great wolfdog.

1.   One of a Kind

He had a good understanding of how people prepared for death. When you make customized gravestones for a living, you run across a lot of peculiar requests. Bob O'Neill and his seven-year old son, Dooley, had just finished laying Agnes Flanagan's marker in St. James Cemetery. Bob stepped back and circled the monument as snow flurries arrived. It appeared to rest solidly on its foundation.

"Dad, how come Mrs. Flanagan wanted her dog's name on the stone next to hers?"

"People have funny wishes, Dooley. Agnes loved Benjie. Even though he died a year before her, she wanted to be sure whoever stopped to visit her here knew how important Benjie was in her life. I guess all dogs should be so lucky. This was a first for me. Well, job's done. Let's head home."

They piled into the aging truck that had carried the monument from Bob's shop. The doors creaked as they closed them. After some sputters and grinding noises, the engine came to life. "The Gray Ghost is feeling her age. She has to hang on one more winter. Then we'll let her retire." He smiled at his son and patted the steering wheel.

Dooley flicked on the radio in time to hear the announcer say, "Looks like old man winter's about to dump a lot of snow on the central New York valley before we say goodbye to 1957. And right on schedule with two days left 'til Christmas. So you still got time to buy that gift for someone special in your life." A few minutes later they pulled into a driveway with a large aluminum mailbox above a small sign: 'Archie Greene, Shepherd Breeding.' Dooley read it and scratched his head beneath a thick wool hat.

"How come we're stopping here?"

Bob looked over at him and put his index finger to his lips. "Can you keep a secret?"

"I guess so." The boy straightened up, turning to face his dad, furrowing his brow.

"I had a little talk with Santa while you were sleeping last night. He told me to come here to get a new addition to our family. An early Christmas present for all of us. He couldn't bring it on his sled so here we are."

"You mean we're gonna get a dog? Holy smokes! Can I pick him out?"

"Let's see what our friend Archie has in his special kennel."

Bob pulled the hulking truck to a stop in front of the sprawling, one story clapboard home. Smoke billowed from a stone chimney. He stepped down from the truck's cabin as the last rays of the sun disappeared behind the surrounding hills. He stretched his arms skyward, arching his back to relieve the tightness and inhaled the cool air through his nostrils before exhaling lingering clouds. The boy jumped down from the passenger's side. The winch on the crane's platform in the truck's bed clanged against its metal mooring.

Bob knocked on the door. A voice from within called, "Come on in. It's open."

Bob filled the entire door frame, ducking slightly to enter the kitchen with his son trailing. Archie Greene, dressed in blue overalls and a flannel shirt, looked up from the table. He took off his bifocals and placed them on the Syracuse Herald Journal, open to the obituaries page. He planted his palms on the table to support himself as he rose slowly to greet his visitors.

"Archie, good to see you, how you holding up?" The two shook equally calloused hands.

"I'm okay, Bob. This weather plays tricks on my knees ever since Korea. Who's this good lookin' fella?"

"That's my number one helper, Dooley." Bob tousled his son's crewcut.

"Nice to meet you, Dooley." Archie's hand swallowed the boy's with a firm grip, something Bob had taught his children was a sign of honesty. "You can hang your coats on the hooks," Archie pointed to the door. "How about some coffee, Bob? Dooley, I bet you like cocoa. What do you say?"

"Sure, thanks, Mr. Greene."

"What brings you two here on a cold December afternoon?"

"Dooley and I were over at St. James Cemetery laying Agnes Flanagan's stone."

"I saw her obituary. Something odd, though, involving her dog."

"Right. About six months before she passed we discussed a special gravestone. She wanted a likeness of Benjie etched into the monument with her smiling at him."

"You must get a lot of strange requests in your line of work. Who knows what crazy ideas people conjure up when they get close to dying?"

Bob sat opposite Archie. Tendrils of steam rose from the hot coffee as he slurped it. His body shook slightly as the jolt of caffeine had its familiar effect.

"I'll tell you, Archie, as we lay that stone today, I got to thinking about a dog for my kids. Agnes and Benjie had a special relationship. She wanted them to be together forever. My kids haven't had a dog they'll remember."

"So you're thinking about a shepherd, huh?" Archie asked as he sipped his coffee, closed the newspaper then shifted his weight away from the stiff left knee.

Bob took another draw on his coffee. "Yeah, I'm thinking a bigger dog is good. Our kids are rough and tumble so we need one that'll hold its own if a couple of 'em try to ride it like a horse. "

Archie clasped his hands inside out to crack his knuckles. "I got a special one out back, unique as they come. He's a Belgian shepherd but got timber wolf in him. His mother went into heat a while back and escaped her pen. Took off for the woods behind me. Must've mated with this wolf that's roamed around here for a while. Not a bad sort." Archie winked at Bob. "Guess he just wanted some company."

Dooley's eyebrows raised in surprise as Bob leaned forward, gripping his mug, focusing on Archie. "This 'wolf-dog,' how old is it?"

"About four weeks, still tiny. Got paws like a lion. Bit of an orphan really. His mama had four pups. He's the only one that survived. The others got diseased, died in a week. Then the mama got hit by a truck and died. This one's got a will to live, that's for sure. Started out giving him baby formula in a bottle. Now he eats and drinks out of a bowl. Dog sees everything, doesn't miss a beat. You wanna go take a look at him?"

"Let's go," Bob said as they rose together, each draining their coffee.

"Leave your coats. I got area heaters out back. The weather turns real fast so I need to make sure the dogs stay warm."

Once in the kennels, they proceeded to a cage where a small black and yellow ball of fur with large pointed ears and enormous paws sat on a thick blanket. Its head turned to watch them approach. At the sight of Archie, the fur ball rose, stretched its limbs and stuck its nose through the wire mesh. Then the small dog looked at Bob.

Bob made eye contact with the dog as Dooley bent down to put his fingers through the widely spaced wire mesh to pet its head. Bob stared at the dog. The dog returned the stare, not diverting its attention to Dooley.

"Like I was saying, this little fella's a needle in a haystack."

As Bob drew closer, the dog lifted its head to catch the man's scent. It gently pawed the wire mesh near where he stood. Bob held the dog's gaze, shook his head and took a deep breath.

Bob knelt next to Dooley and the dog moved to him and licked his hand as Bob caressed its head. Dooley watched his father quiver slightly. The puppy closed its eyes as it absorbed Bob's scent.

"Dad, we should take him home. I think he likes us. And he keeps staring at you like he knows you. Mrs. Bennett said in school last week that some countries believe in reincar-something. It's where people die and come back as animals. Maybe this dog knew you before."

"Yes, reincarnation. Who knows, maybe this little fella was someone we knew once. He sure seems to be talking to us. "

Archie broke in. "Well, that's about the sum of it. This dog's different but in the end he'll make some family a fine companion. So, if you want him, it's $30."

Bob reached into his pocket, "Here's $40. It's Christmas. We'll take good care of this little guy." Archie opened the gate and the small wolfdog immediately went to Bob, jumping with both front legs trying to climb him. Bob lowered his hand to pet the dog's head, and the puppy licked it repeatedly.

"Bob, you must have a way with dogs. He likes my wife and me just fine, but he treats you like royalty. I was worried about finding him a good home. Some people don't like the wolf part, you know. "

"This dog seems to be talking to me. And I'm understanding. Maybe it's the magic of Christmas. I don't know. Anyway, Betty and the kids are in for a big surprise."

Bob picked up the small fur ball and cuddled him in his big arms. Dooley continued to stroke its back. The four of them returned to the warm kitchen. Dooley zipped up his woolen coat then Bob handed the animal to him. Bob put on his big coat and particles of stone dust flew off into the air.

"Well, Betty will be wondering where we are. I had no idea what to expect when we pulled into your driveway. This little fella will be a welcome addition to the family."

Archie smiled. "I'm sure he will. By the way, let me give you some dog food to last you 'til you get to the store. Start him off with a cup in the morning and another at night then double it after each thirty pounds he grows."

"How big you think he'll get?"

"Looking at those paws, probably a hundred thirty, easy. His mama was about that."

"Archie, have a good Christmas."

"You, too, Bob."

Outside, they watched the puppy lift his head to smell the air and feel the snowflakes and cool breeze against his face. Once inside the Gray Ghost, he nestled between the two of them then jumped a little as Bob urged the old Dodge's engine to lumber to life. As they drove back toward Route 20, Bob sang 'Have Yourself A Merry Little Christmas.'

"Dad, what do you think we should call him?"

Bob scratched his chin and looked down at the dog. "What do you think about Archie? He led us to this young fella."

Dooley nodded. "Yeah, I like that." He gently petted their passenger. "What do you think, Archie?" The dog looked up at him and perked its ears erect. "I think he likes it!"

Thirty minutes later they passed a sign, 'entering the village of Cazenovia.' "Archie, welcome home," Bob said. "You're Cazenovia's newest citizen."

"Dad, I think he's going to like living here. Wait 'til the kids see him. And mom's in for a big surprise, too, right?"

Bob nodded. "I think a lot of people are in for a surprise. Let's hope your mom thinks so too."

They turned down Sullivan Street, headed toward the village green then pulled into a gravel driveway next to a brown shingled house with a sagging roof over the porch that circled the front and side. Bob cut the motor, which spit out a few coughs before it eventually silenced.

"Let's pull a little surprise on mom and the kids, what do you think?"

Dooley wrinkled his brow in a quizzical way. Bob lowered himself from the cab, reached in and gently picked up Archie and put him inside his coat so the dog was hidden.

"Now, Dooley, don't say anything when we walk in. We'll tell mom we got delayed a little at the graveyard."

Archie instinctively reacted to being placed in cramped quarters by trying to escape but Bob looked in his eyes, petted his head and put his index finger to his lips for Archie to be quiet. Archie complied. They stamped their boots outside the front door to remove snow then walked into a noisy greeting from four young voices.

Ten year-old Bob junior looked up from the Lincoln Logs fort he was building with four-year old Patrick. The Irish twins, Maureen and Lisa, born 14 months apart, stood in their playpen nearby watching the sudden burst of activity. Betty O'Neill emerged from the kitchen wearing a print apron and a look of exasperation.

"Bob, where have you been? Dinner's been ready for over an hour."

"Well, Dooley and I had to spend a little extra time laying Agnes Flanagan's stone. We think she'll be happy with it looking down from heaven, right Dooley?"

"Oh, sure, Dad. Mrs. Flanagan will be real happy. That stone has a carving of her and her dog on it, just like she wanted. Everybody loves dogs." He smirked a little.

"Daddy, why is your coat moving?" asked Patrick, looking in earnest at Bob's coat that showed sudden, errant bulges.

"Well, we have a little surprise. Anyone want to guess what's in there?"

"Is it something from Santa, Dad?" asked Bob junior, who was on the cusp of not believing in the great bearded man.

"Yes, it is."

Maureen, meanwhile, who recently had begun to speak, blurted from the playpen, "It a toy."

"Not quite, but it can make noises."

Just then, Archie squirmed and stuck out his head from the coat, gazed in all directions and let out a yap. A stunned moment of silence preceded a chorus of joy as small hands gravitated from all directions toward Bob's coat.

"A puppy, a puppy, can I hold him? What's his name? Where did he come from?"

Betty leaned up against the doorway, a look of complete surprise crossing her face. Bob lifted Archie aloft, then held out a hand calling for quiet. The kids stood in rapt attention like little soldiers. Dooley smiled like a Cheshire cat. Betty remained silent, stunned at the sudden appearance of the dog.

Bob waited until everyone settled down. "Kids, this is Archie. Santa visited me and told me to make an early delivery. Archie is a very special new member of our family. He's unique because his father was a wolf and his mother was a dog. Wolves are very smart. They have to survive in the wilderness." Betty shivered at the word 'wolf.'

"Daddy", Patrick chimed in, "we talked about wolves in school. They don't eat people. Only the one in Red Riding Hood does that. They like to eat rabbits. What about him? Does he eat rabbits too?"

"No, Archie is mostly dog with some wolf in him. He eats dog food. You're going to discover that he is very smart. When Dooley and I were picking him out, Archie was talking to me with his eyes. He told me he is so happy to be a part of this family."

Everyone stared at Bob. Patrick looked quizzically at his father. "Daddy, how can a dog talk to you? I never heard one talk. They just bark. Is Archie a magic dog?"

"Yes, Archie is a magic dog. For right now, he just talks to me. So I'll have to interpret what he says." All the children, except young Bob, nodded. They knew about fairy tales and believed in magic.

Dooley stepped forward to pet Archie. "Dad told me on the way to get Archie that Santa said he didn't have room on his sled for Archie so that's why we got him early. Santa thinks of everything. And then, when dad and Archie first saw each other, it was like they were old friends."

Young Bob looked down at his feet and covered his mouth with his hand to hide a smile. Patrick and the girls looked wide-eyed at Dooley.

Big Bob gently stroked Archie. "If you love him, he will love you back. In a few months though, Archie will become very big, much bigger than any of you. He's going to need all our help to grow up. Do all of you think you can teach Archie right from wrong?"

"We'll take care of him, Dad," Bob junior confidently stated.

"You can count on us, Dad," Dooley said, reinforcing his older brother. Patrick, eyes wide, trying to absorb what was happening, silently nodded, agreeing to something he did not remotely understand. The infant and toddler sisters squealed with joy. Something new and good was happening, enough to celebrate by screaming happily. Betty, her face getting redder, had bided her time, waiting for a small break in the celebration to speak.

"Bob, when did you decide it was a good time to get a dog? Isn't this a decision we should have discussed? Don't you think five kids are enough responsibility for the two of us? You're gone God knows where and now I have two in diapers and a four-legged new one to toilet train. Not to mention the expense of a dog, food, vet bills. Things are tight as it is. I wish you had talked with me first."

"Mom, don't worry, we know what to do," her older boys said almost in unison. Her shoulders slumped and she exhaled, blowing away the hair on her forehead.

"Betty, I'm telling you this is a special dog. Believe it or not, Archie can communicate to people. I swear it's destiny he found this family."

Betty shook her head. "Sometimes I think I'm living with six children. Anyway, dinner already is cold and this one," pointing an accusatory finger at Archie, "probably has to eat too."

Big Bob lowered the puppy to the floor as the three boys surrounded Archie. The girls squealed happily from the playpen as Betty lowered Maureen to the floor and picked up Lisa whose legs were pumping like pistons. Enveloped in young hands stroking his entire body, Archie looked up at big Bob. The entourage proceeded into the kitchen. Bob junior collected from the doorway a bag Dooley had carried into the house.

"I'll feed Archie, Dad. How much of this food do I give him?"

A cup twice a day until he grows more. Then we can increase it. I'll let you know when."

Bob junior placed a bowl of food and water in the pantry. Archie delicately ate it then lay down next to Big Bob's feet at the head of the table. Three seated boys and two girls in highchairs stared at the dog as Betty encouraged them to finish their vegetables. Through the window next to the lit Christmas tree in the den, large snowflakes descended, foreshadowing a white Christmas.

2.   The Dispute

"Bob, this little guy is going to be a handful when he fills out," Dr. Armstrong, the veterinarian, said as he examined Archie and vaccinated him. "How long have you had him?"

Three weeks, Bill." Young Bob and Dooley stood next to Archie, stroking his back and head. "He's been gaining about three pounds a week."

The veterinarian examined the dog's legs and hips then turned to Big Bob. "Have you started to leash train him and what about his bathroom habits?"

"You know, he follows orders like a soldier at boot camp. I haven't even bought a leash. And as far as his peeing and pooping, he hasn't gone once in the house."

"Yeah," Dooley interjected giggling, "Archie goes behind Eddie Fiedler's house in the woods. They probably don't even know. He never goes on our lawn. And guess what? Bob and I walk him around town and he just follows us. We went into a store and told Archie to wait outside. And he did!"

"Very unusual for a dog this young to follow directions and not take off after some cat or squirrel. Most people I see keep puppies on a leash for six months before they follow commands."

"Maybe it's the wolf in him," young Bob offered, "Dad says they're real smart 'cause they have to survive in the wilderness."

The veterinarian turned to the boy with a puzzled look. "He's a Belgian shepherd, son. The police train them due to their high intelligence. Why do you say wolf?"

Big Bob intervened. "We got him from Archie Greene. He said our dog's mother got pregnant from a timber wolf that hangs around in the woods behind his kennel. A few weeks later she got hit by a car chasing a fox and didn't make it. None of the other pups in the litter survived—just Archie. Somehow, he had the will to live."

"Yes, Archie raises nice shepherds. I've gotta say, this is the first time I ever encountered a shepherd with wolf lineage. Very unusual. Well, the ears are pure shepherd, and the hips are spaced like some of the larger ones I've seen. Not sure about the wolf, except..." He examined Archie's muzzle, snout, and finally peered directly at Archie's unblinking eyes. "There's the wolf."

"How big you think he'll get, Bill?"

"Judging from the size of those paws, you're looking at probably 120, 130 pounds. Not many other dogs will want to tangle with him. With regular exercise and a good diet, he'll grow at a steady pace and be healthy."

"So, nothing unusual about him?"

"Not really. Although take a look at this." Armstrong pried open Archie's mouth, as Archie squirmed against the pressure from the vet's hands. "Never seen that before. A large black circle in the middle of his tongue. Nothing wrong with it, just an odd birthmark. You'll always know he's your dog by looking at that mark. He's good to go. See you in a year for a check-up."

Outside the sun dipped over the horizon as they buttoned their coats to brace against a chill wind. Archie followed them to the Gray Ghost and waited to be lifted into the cab. The ancient truck's engine resisted starting but eventually kicked over.

"Boys, let's go home and see how mom and the kids are doing." They rode in silence. Archie curled himself into a ball and fell asleep between Dooley and his father.

Twenty minutes later they pulled into One Union Street. Dooley lifted Archie from the cab. The dog wandered near a shriveled bush next to the garage to pee. "Good boy, Archie," Dooley said, as he pranced toward the boys and rubbed up against their legs.

"Did Bill say anything about him being dangerous because of the wolf part?" Betty emerged in her usual print apron from the kitchen, her eyebrows knitted in a frown. The Irish twins squealed with delight from the playpen in the living room.

Patrick put down his crayons and coloring book, approached Archie and gently stroked the dog's head. Archie sat facing him and licked Patrick's chin. "That tickles," Patrick chortled.

"Nothing unusual, Betty, our young friend is going to be just fine. Nothing for us to worry about." Bob glanced at his wife quickly, then turned his attention to his children, smiling as the boys played with their new family member.

"Yeah, Mom, and guess what? Archie has a black mark on his tongue so we'll always know he's ours," Dooley announced like a knowledgeable scientist. "Look at this, "he continued, wrestling Archie to the floor, prying open his jaws.

"Dooley, I believe you. Let's not get him excited," Betty cautioned. "We don't want him biting anyone. He's still on probation."

Dooley furrowed his brow. "What's that mean –pro-bration?"

"It's pro-ba-tion," she enunciated. "That means as long as Archie behaves he can stay. If he turns into a bad boy, he goes. After all, he's part wolf. We don't want him biting anybody. That would be a big problem."

An uncomfortable silence engulfed the entryway.

Breaking the momentary tenseness in the air, young Bob implored, "We'll make sure he behaves, Mom. So far, so good, right?"

Big Bob backed up his oldest son. "You and Dooley are taking great care of our young friend. And Patrick will help out too when he gets a little older. Right, Patrick?" His eyes wide open and mystified over the meaning of this future commitment, he silently nodded.

Bob glared at his wife. She did not turn away. "Look, Bob, let's not kid ourselves. He looks like a cute puppy today. What happens when he's big and the wolf wildness comes out in him? You're going to be pretty upset if he bites one of your children and he has to be put down." The three boys stared at their mother, their mouths open, eyes wide and unblinking.

"Betty, Archie won't do that. He's special. I'm positive. Give him a chance."

"All right. I give up, for now. Dinner's almost ready. You boys go wash your hands." Betty turned to her husband and in a low voice said, "We'll talk about this when the kids are asleep." She turned on her heels and headed into the kitchen. Dinner proceeded in silence.

After dinner, Bob drove to the store. The two older boys cleaned the dishes then walked Archie around the neighborhood. After she put the Irish twins to bed, Betty came downstairs and found young Bob and Dooley playing with the dog in the den. The phone, the only one in the house, rang a few feet away in the kitchen and Betty answered it. The boys looked up at their mother who had her back turned to them.

"Hello. Yes, I have a few minutes Mrs. Driscoll." As two minutes passed, Betty leaned against the wall and rubbed her forehead with the hand not holding the phone. "Mrs. Driscoll, I will speak with Bob. We'll find a way to solve this. There's no need to resort to contacting a bill collector." She hung up and shook her head.

Bob approached his mother. "Mom, you okay? Your face is all red."

"I'll be fine dear."

"Who was that on the phone?"

"It's just grownup discussion. Your father and I will speak about it later. You and Dooley can watch a show and then it's time for bed. Is your homework done?" Bob nodded.

Later that night, the kids tucked in, Bob and Betty sat at the kitchen table, out of range of curious young ears. Archie curled up on his blanket in the corner of the den. His presence featured front and center in the adults' discussion. Dooley, meanwhile, had slipped downstairs for a glass of milk and stayed in the den out of sight when he heard his parents' voices in a tone he had heard before, one that told him to stay away.

"Bob, just what were you thinking when you got this dog? Sometimes I think you live in a dream world. Do you think money grows on trees? How do we pay the heating bill? Mike Driscoll has carried us three months but he has a business to run. I don't know what you agreed with him. His wife called me while you were out, threatening to contact a collection agency if we don't pay by the middle of the month. She is an awful woman. I felt embarrassed talking with her."

"Betty, just be patient. I'll talk to Mike. He knows my business has ups and downs. He realizes I'll make him whole once I get more work. I'm just having a little bad luck right now."

"Well, your bad luck just gets worse. What happens when your truck dies? It's on life support. And when someone does pay you, off you go to Albert's to buy drinks for your friends. We have five mouths to feed and now a sixth who needs food and vet services. Maybe you need a different job. My brother Jim could help you get an insurance job. Talk to him."

"Listen, give me a few months to get out of this rut. I know I can make a living with monuments and it's what I'm good at. If it doesn't work out by summer, I'll call Jim."

"And this dog, what were you thinking? What if he bites somebody? He's got wolf in him for heaven's sakes. We could get sued and lose everything. Stop and think. Your actions have consequences for us." She looked down at her dress, folded a wrinkle and shook her head.

"Give Archie the benefit of the doubt. I swear he's a special dog. When I saw him, I felt tingles down my spine, like he was talking to me through his eyes. Never experienced anything like it. He's going to be good for our kids. I just know it."

Betty's chair scraped along the kitchen floor as she stood and began waving her hands. "I can't believe what I'm hearing. Archie talks and you listen. Are you crazy? I've had a long day. I hope you know what you're doing. This family needs some sanity right now and I think I'm the only sane adult in this house."

Dooley abandoned his urge for milk, tiptoed through the dining room and up the stairs to his bedroom. He pulled the blanket up to his chin, turning his head away from the door and feigning sleep. Before leaving the kitchen, Betty gave her husband a long, hard stare. Bob poured himself a coffee. As Betty passed the den, Archie's ears perked up and he looked into the kitchen at Bob. He got up from his blanket, yawned, stretched the length of his body and approached the kitchen table. He sat next to Bob who massaged Archie's ears.

Bob's two hands cupped Archie's head beneath the dog's jaw. He stared deeply into Archie's eyes. "Archie, great wolfdog, if you can understand me, listen carefully. You have an important role in

THE DISPUTE

this family to protect your brothers and sisters. You are young but I believe you know what you have to do. We have a long journey ahead. Now, go to sleep my friend."

Archie's ears perked up, he looked in Bob's eyes, licked his master's hand then returned to his blanket, curling himself into a ball. Bob drained his coffee, turned off the lights and headed to the couch in the living room where he stripped to his underwear, turned off the end table light and pulled the afghan over him.

3.   A Day in the Life

The three boys bolted through the front door in mid-afternoon, yelled "Hi, Mom, we're home" in unison, then made a beeline for Archie. Bob and Dooley vigorously hugged him as Patrick smiled from a few feet away. Archie licked their faces as they wrestled with him. Betty stood in the kitchen doorway with arms crossed.

"Boys, how was school today?"

"Yeah, it was good, Mom." The boys continued playing with Archie. "How about you, boy? Did you have fun today?"

Betty glared at the big puppy and pursed her lips. "If 'having fun' means getting in my way all day when I have things to do, then, yes, he had a marvelous day. Maybe you boys could teach him not to follow me around the house while you're at school. Or maybe your father could since he seems to have this magical way of talking to the dog." Betty's crossed her arms and shook her head while frowning. "I have things to do. He drops a ball at my feet or sits next to me when I knit. Then he tries to put his paw on my knee. I just don't have time for that. I tell him to go lie down. Then, when I bring the girls down from their nap, he gets them excited and stands near the playpen. I'm afraid he'll bite their hands if they stick them near his mouth."

Dooley smiled at her as he wrapped his arms around the dog's midsection and pulled him to the floor. Archie tried to wrestle free. "He'd never bite us, Mom. He loves us. Can't you tell?"

Patrick had stood off to the side quietly observing the discussion. As Dooley let go of Archie, he approached the dog and ever so gently like a feather ran his hand over Archie's snout and face. For a moment silence ruled with Patrick and Archie center stage. "Nice puppy," Patrick said in a hushed tone.

Betty watched her youngest son for a moment, mesmerized at how affectionate he and Archie appeared toward each other. Then she shook her head slightly. "Kids, remember, this dog is young and part of him is wolf. Who knows what he's capable of doing." The boys looked at their mother with quizzical expressions. "Anyway, Bob, it's time for you and Dooley to do the paper route. Patrick, did Mrs. Stewart give you any homework?" He nodded silently and Betty pointed to the couch in the living room.

Archie, now nearing eighty pounds, trailed Bob and Dooley who rode their bikes the four blocks to Ryan's Funeral Home where they collected seventy copies of the Syracuse Herald Journal, folded them with rubber bands then loaded the papers into the oversized basket attached to Bob's handlebars.

"Archie, here, boy, take this to that door." Bob pointed as he knelt near the dog and put a newspaper in Archie's mouth. Dooley stood next to Bob's bike and extracted a paper as he watched them. Archie just stood there not moving. Bob led him to the porch steps and pointed to the place mat. Archie bounded up the steps and dropped the paper on the mat, turned and looked at Bob, ears perked straight up. Dooley put the paper under his arm and clapped.

"Good boy, Archie," Bob congratulated their assistant as he and Dooley hugged the dog. Every few houses they repeated the process. At some homes, the three of them went to the front door and rang the bell. Bob removed from his back pocket a small green book with names down the left column and dates across the top. He pulled a stubby pencil from his shirt pocket. A woman in her forties came to the door. "Hi, Mrs. Dougherty, we're collecting for the week. That's sixty cents."

"Hang on a second, boys, let me get my purse." Jean Dougherty returned a minute later with three quarters, two lollipops and a milk bone dog biscuit. "Here you go. Bob, you keep the difference. You boys are doing a good job delivering our paper. And Archie seems quite the valuable helper. I see him along with you boys rain or shine. So here's a little treat for each of you."

"Gee, thanks Mrs. Dougherty," Bob said as Dooley nodded.

Three doors down lived widower Joe Bobette, ninety-four years old, who kept himself in superb physical condition. He liked to tell stories of battles he fought in World War I. He was fond of telling the boys how Archie reminded him of "war dogs" the troops had who helped locate wounded soldiers. As the three of them approached Joe's door, Bob looked at Dooley. "It's your turn."

"I thought I did it last time," Dooley said holding his palms up.

"Nope, he got me in fifty-five seconds. He said it was a new record. Look, he gives us a forty cent tip every week. Just deal with it." The younger brother shook his head as he pounded the lion's head door knocker against its brass base.

Moments later, the door opened and a man about five foot six inches tall with a slight build and wisp of white hair peeking out of his scalp smiled at the boys. He wore a long sleeve white shirt and suspenders holding up gray slacks. "Well, well, well, who do we have here? My favorite paperboys and the world's only paper delivery dog. Come on in. Who is my victim today?"

"It's me, this time, Mr. Bobette. But you told me last time that I get to pick offense or defense. So I pick offense this time, okay?"

"Pick your poison, Dooley," Joe Bobette said with a smile as he moved aside a coffee table in the ancient living room to create a large open space before he knelt down on all fours. "The 1878 Onondaga County one hundred forty-five pound class wrestling champion is ready for you."

The boy knelt perpendicular to Joe, left hand on Joe's left elbow and right arm wrapped around the old man's waist. Archie circled the duo, occasionally sticking his head close to sniff them. Bob looked at the clock over the fireplace mantle. "All right, twenty seconds to the signal. Ready... set.... wrestle!"

Despite his age, Joe knew all the tricks. He grabbed Dooley's right hand, stuck out his right leg and rolled backward, catching the boy off balance. Within moments he had him in a half-nelson and thirty seconds later both of Dooley's shoulder blades remained in contact with the Oriental rug for the required three seconds. Archie circled the action wagging his tail and barking.

"Pinned!" Bob yelled.

"Time?" Joe asked.

"A minute seven," Bob replied.

Joe looked at his adversary. They were both panting with faces red. Dooley rose and stood next to Archie. "Not bad, young man. We'll make a wrestler out of you yet. How about a ginger ale, boys?"

They retreated into the kitchen where Joe handed the boys bottles of Canada Dry Ginger Ale and he placed a bowl of water on the floor for Archie. Joe handed Bob a crisp dollar bill. The boy thanked him and placed it in the collection pouch attached to his belt. Joe approached Archie and rubbed the dog's ears. He sat down in his chair, sipped his ginger ale and rubbed his chin as he stared at the dog.

"You know, boys, if I didn't know any better, I'd say your buddy here has wolf in him. He sure has the eyes of one." The boys stared at each other and raised their eyebrows then shrugged their shoulders.

Bob replied after a momentary silence. "Maybe he does have something wild in him, Mr. Bobette. He's still growing and even though he's a puppy, he's plenty smart. He already delivered about twenty papers today. Those are his houses. Sure makes our job go faster." Dooley nodded. "Well, we have to get going. Thanks for the soda and for the tip. Maybe when Archie's full grown, you can wrestle him!" All three of them laughed as Archie circled them.

"Boys, when this young fella's full grown, I don't think I'd want to tangle with him. As long as Archie is with you, I think you'll be well protected. Okay, see you next week."

The shadows along Sullivan Street were lengthening as they finished the last few houses on the route. Just down the block from their home they knocked on Alice Laurel's door. She answered it with eighteen-month old Janie in her arms. Just then her phone rang. "Oh, here, Bob, have a seat and hold Janie, will you? I'll get that call."

Bob sat with the toddler on his lap as Dooley stood nearby. Archie approached Bob to sniff the baby. Janie gurgled some words and squealed with delight, reaching out to touch Archie's muzzle with her chubby little hands as Archie licked her bare leg. Alice returned and laughed at the sight. "Bob, do you think I can hire Archie as a babysitter? Janie appears to like him a lot more than some of the others I have." She took her baby as she handed Bob some coins.

Thanks, Mrs. Laurel, see you next week. As far as babysitting, it might be a while. Archie's only about six months old."

"Well, he sure is a nice dog. You must be doing something right raising him."

Big Bob pulled in the driveway as the boys returned home. Archie bounded over to him and rubbed up against the man's legs. Bob engulfed the dog's head in his hands as he looked at his sons. "How's your four-legged assistant doing these days? A lot of your customers must know him by now."

Dooley stepped forward and put his arm around Archie's neck. "Archie makes the job go faster. We have him deliver the paper to certain houses so he understands what to do. Some people give him a biscuit. Everybody likes him. He even goes into the stores downtown."

Bob returned from putting his bike in the garage and stood next to his father. "You know Mr. Evans, right, the guy who works at Aikman's Hardware?" Big Bob nodded. "Well, he talked with me about the Boy Scouts on account of he's scoutmaster for Troop 18. He said when I turn 11 this December I could join. And get this, he said Archie could be troop mascot! He can go to all the meetings, even our campouts."

Big Bob put his hand on his son's shoulder. "Archie's getting to be on a first name basis with a lot of people."

"Yeah, and people aren't afraid of him. We haven't told anyone he's part wolf. We figure they don't need to know. Like, Mr. Bobette, for instance. He told us today he thinks Archie might be part wolf. We didn't say yes or no, right Dooley?" His brother nodded. "Archie is friendly to everybody and he learns stuff fast. It's like he understands what we say."

Big Bob smiled at the boys and the dog. "Boys, Archie is just going to get smarter. He is a special dog. Come on, let's see what mom has cooked up for dinner."

The next morning Archie rose with Big Bob near six. Bob turned on the gas stove to heat water for coffee then let out Archie for his morning constitutional in the woods behind Fiedler's house. Bob fed Archie breakfast before finishing his coffee.

They sat alone in the kitchen awaiting the procession of young footsteps clambering down the stairs seeking cereal. Dooley was the first of the kids to rise and rubbed his eyes as he descended into the kitchen as his father, sitting with his back toward the doorway, spoke to Archie.

"Great wolf-dog," Bob gently spoke as he looked deeply in Archie's brown eyes. "What is on your agenda today?" Archie stared at his master, tilting his big head first left, then right before placing a paw on Bob's knee. "Perhaps some more exploring since I understand from some friends that you have become a frequent visitor to them."

"That's for sure, Dad," Dooley said as he approached his father and the man engulfed the boy in his arms. Dooley knelt down to hug Archie.

"Well, Dooley, I have my own agenda today so I better get dressed and get a move on. I think I hear the troops coming downstairs now."

After the kids finished their morning cereal, the boys placed their bowls on the floor and Archie drank the milk and any Cheerios stuck to the side. Young Bob convinced Betty that Archie should accompany the boys to school. She appeared fine with the idea. "Anything that gets that dog out from under my feet is good. Just check with Mr. Schumard to see if he's okay with your dog staying near school while you're there. And for heaven's sakes, don't say anything about him being part wolf." So, Archie accompanied the boys to school. Bob and Dooley got the principal's permission for Archie to sit outside the door of the elementary building. It helped that Archie delivered the newspaper to both Bob Schumard and his secretary.

Later that night, as Bob and Dooley lay in twin beds in their room they spoke in hushed tones about the day's events and what tomorrow would bring. They heard steps approaching and pulled up the covers to their chins and pretended to be asleep. The door opened slightly and then closed.

Mike whispered, turning his head toward his brother, "You know, the funniest thing happened. Dad told me he was driving past the school in the middle of the morning on the way to the cemetery when he saw Archie walking across the green heading for downtown. Instead of calling him, dad decided to park the truck and follow him. It was like he was spying on Archie.

"He told me he followed at a distance so Archie wouldn't smell him. Archie went to the back door of Smith's Market and barked a couple of times. Bucky Bennett, the butcher guy, he came out and gave Archie a small bone. Then, a few minutes later, dad said Archie scratched at the back door of Aikman's until Art Evans let him in. Dad snuck a peek through the back window and saw

Archie and Art having a good time. Then Art gave him a milk bone dog biscuit."

Bob chuckled. "Doesn't sound like Archie's starving."

"Yeah, for sure. Then dad said Art let Archie out the front door. So dad went around to the front in time to see Archie cross the street to Theobald's Drug Store. He said Archie even turned his head to wait for a car to pass before he crossed. How does he know how to do that stuff?"

"I don't know. He's just wicked smart, I guess."

"Well, by then dad figured he better talk with these people Archie was seeing. They all told dad he visits them every day. What's up with that?"

"So, what did they do then?" Bob asked.

"After that, dad just let Archie lead him wherever Archie wanted to go. Archie went down to the lake for a drink before heading back to school. Dad said Archie just went back to the front door and laid down. Well, he's always there when we leave at noon to go home for lunch, right?"

Bob nodded. "Wow, I never realized Archie did all that stuff. I mean, I know people like him. But when you think about it, he's really like the whole town's dog. I bet if he could talk, he could run for mayor of Cazenovia and win!" The boys giggled, pulled up the blankets and fell asleep.

As usual, Archie awaited the three boys at noon at the school's entrance. They walked home with Archie circling them and brushing up against their legs as they skipped along the sidewalk. For lunch, they always ate peanut butter and jelly sandwiches. Betty happened to be out with the girls. Patrick never finished his sandwich so Archie knew to sit right next to him. He pulled the crusts off and ate the center and gave what he didn't want to Archie in small morsels. Archie knew not to look to Dooley, who never provided leftovers.

Patrick looked at his older brothers. "Mom says dogs get sick from peanut butter, but Archie really likes it. I never saw him get sick. He's still kind of a baby puppy. The sandwiches will help him grow up." Patrick nodded confidently.

Bob looked at his brothers then at the clock on the wall. "Your secret's safe with me, Patrick. And I don't think Archie is gonna squeal to mom." The boys giggled collectively. Dooley held his hand to his mouth as purple colored peanut butter creeped out the side. "Okay, guys, we got to get a move on. The lunch hour bell is gonna ring in ten minutes."

The boys took the shortcut to school through the Anderson's backyard, a route they reserved for when they needed a faster path. They didn't use it all the time as Mr. Anderson yelled at them if he saw them on his lawn. They slithered through a hole in the tall chain link fence on the back of the property that bordered the school. It was wide enough for Archie to slip through. They hurried to the front door, bade Archie farewell and went to their respective classrooms. Three hours later as school let out, Archie was right where they left him. They wondered aloud to each other as they walked home what adventures Archie might have done that afternoon.

4.   Lost

"Dooley, leave enough Cheerios for everyone. Don't put them in a mixing bowl. Use a regular bowl." He stared back at his mother, looked down at the big bowl, then grimaced slightly before extracting a cereal bowl from the cupboard. The Irish twins babbled away in matching highchairs throwing cheerios toward a grateful Archie. "Kids," Betty continued, "This Saturday we're going to Shopping Town to buy new shoes for school."

"Can Archie come?" asked newly minted five-year old Patrick. "He's never been outside of Cazenovia. Maybe he should see someplace else. "

"I don't think that's a good idea, honey. Archie would just have to sit in the car while we're in the store. He's better off here."

"He's never been left alone, Mom," interjected Dooley. "Even when we go to church he waits outside St. James for us."

"People leave dogs home alone all the time. He'll be fine."

"Yeah, but this could be an adventure for him."

Betty lowered her head and paused before saying, "He'll be fine here."

On Saturday morning Betty loaded the five kids into the 1953 Chevy wagon with matching rust marks front and back. Like the

Gray Ghost, it sounded sick but it ran. The kids waved to Archie looking at them from the dining room window, ears straight up and long tongue hanging down, front paws on the window sill, as they pulled out of the driveway. Betty took back roads to Shopping Town. About two miles from their house, Dooley looked out the back window and screamed.

"Mom, mom, stop the car! Archie's running behind us. A car will hit him."

"Oh, dear God, how did that dog get out of the house?" She looked in her rearview mirror and kept driving. "Well, he'll get tired of running and just turn around and go home."

Bob, Patrick and Dooley shouted at her in unison. "Mom, you have to stop. He doesn't know where to go! He'll get hurt or lost. He has to come with us!" The Irish twins screamed at the sudden excitement. Patrick started crying. Betty slowed down and rubbed her forehead but hesitated stopping. She glanced at the two kids in front and the others in the back seat that were kneeling looking out the back window. All were in hysterics.

"Archie's gonna die," Patrick moaned. "He needs to come with us. He's just a puppy. Mom, please let him in." The noise inside the car suddenly subsided as Betty pulled over. Archie, tongue hanging almost to the ground, bolted the final half mile to them as

LOST

Bob got out the passenger door. The kids clapped and rejoiced as the car came to a halt. Patrick stopped crying.

"It's okay boy, you're with us now." Bob knelt to welcome a heavily panting Archie, who flew into Bob's arms. Bob hugged him hard.

Betty looked at Archie through the open passenger door and shook her head. The dog, chest heaving, looked at her without reacting. Betty checked for cars in both directions then got out, opening the tailgate. "Put him in the back. He's coming with us after all. He'll have to stay in the car."

During the ride to Shopping Town, the kids in back petted Archie, congratulating him for tracking them down. Bob turned to his mother. "Mom, that was the right thing to do. Archie wasn't going to turn around and go home. He'll be okay in the car. He's just not used to being alone."

"I don't understand why he has to go everywhere with us. He's a dog. Well, he's part dog and part dangerous wolf. Why can't he act like other dogs and just stay put like he's supposed to?"

In the parking lot, Betty instructed the older boys to leave the windows down part way so Archie could get some fresh air. Bob put the front windows down halfway and Dooley did the same to the back windows. "Dooley, take Patrick's hand, there are lots of cars around here." Before rounding the corner for Penney's department store, the kids looked back at Archie. His head was out the back window with the long tongue hanging down.

"Look, kids, we'll just be an hour. He'll be fine. Stop worrying about him. He's a dog. People leave dogs alone in a lot of places. He just has to learn that he can't go everywhere we go." She shook her head and quickened her pace with Lisa in her arms and Maureen being dragged by the hand.

An hour later Betty and the kids headed for the car. Dooley held Patrick's hand with a bag of shoe boxes in the other hand. Bob had bags of shoe boxes in both hands. Betty walked with the Irish Twins keeping an eye on the parking lot. Betty looked down at her kids. "You were all very good in the store. We'll stop at Lipes Dairy and get an ice cream cone on the way home. Now, be careful here. There are a lot of cars in this lot so stay with me."

Patrick looked at his mother. "Mom, can we get Archie and ice cream cone too? He was a good boy waiting in the car."

"I suppose so, Patrick. I hope he behaved and didn't claw the seats or bother people by barking."

As they approached the car, they saw it was empty. Archie had vanished. The kids immediately panicked. Patrick and Dooley ran to the nearby corner of the parking lot, cupping their hands, calling "Archie, Archie." Bob dropped the boxes and ran in an opposite direction calling the dog's name. Betty, shouted at her boys to return. "Boys, do not run in this parking lot. Cars are moving all the time. Get back here. We will find your dog." Betty put the Irish Twins in the back seat and placed her right hand over her brow and scanned the horizon. Nothing.

Dooley, on the verge of tears, looked up at his mother and put his hands on her shoulders. "What are we gonna do? Archie's gone. We have to find him, now!"

Betty looked around making certain all her kids were by the car. She put both hands to her face and rubbed her eyes. She spotted a policeman in front of a paint store and pointed toward him. "Let's go talk to him, kids." She took the girls from the back seat then led her troop to the policeman. The boys bolted to the officer and immediately started to talk over one another to him until he held up both hands and looked at Betty.

"Ma'am, what seems to be the problem here?"

"Officer, our seven-month old German shepherd somehow got out of our car. His name is Archie and this is the first time he's ever been outside of Cazenovia where we live."

"Ma'am, were your doors locked?"

"It doesn't matter, really because we left the windows down halfway. He's too big to climb out. He weighs probably 80 pounds. Maybe someone stole him, I don't know."

"I'll call this in. We'll have patrolmen on the lookout for him. Was he wearing a collar with his name on it? And does he have any distinguishing features?"

"He wasn't wearing a collar, that I know. Where we live most dogs don't wear collars."

Dooley tugged the policeman's elbow. "Sir, he has a big black spot in the middle of his tongue. You could recognize him from that. The animal doctor said it was unique."

"Well, that will help confirm his identity if we get close enough to catch him. Is there some reason someone would want to steal him?"

Again, Dooley chirped in. "He's part wolf. His mother had babies with a real wolf. Does that make him valuable?"

Betty rolled her eyes at this statement, then shook her head.

"Wait a minute, ma'am. Did your son say your dog is part wolf? Has he bitten anyone to your knowledge? If so, he could be a danger to society and that's a totally different issue."

"No, nothing like that, officer. Archie has wolf lineage but he's no danger to anyone. Do you think I would have a dangerous animal living with these young children?" Betty paused and silently stared at the policeman who scanned the young assembly. He backed off.

"Okay. Let me get some information from you and we'll see what we can do. He's not likely to turn up at your house. That's 17 miles from here. And you say he's never been outside of Cazenovia?"

"That's right. He's never been away from us."

"Do you have a picture of him? Anything recent?"

"I'll have to see what we have at home. My husband will bring you something. Is that your station off of Fayetteville road?" Betty's arms were tiring from holding Lisa in one arm and Maureen's hand with the other. The three boys were asking many questions at the same time. The young policeman looked from her to them and back to her. Passers-by frowned at the scene.

"Yes. Someone is there around the clock. The sooner we get something on your dog, the better chance we have of locating him. I don't want to sound too pessimistic but you do realize this is a congested traffic area. Delivery trucks are everywhere. Let's hope he sticks to back streets."

Dooley and Bob looked at each other and frowned. "Mom," Bob looked at his mother, "We don't have a lot of trucks in Cazenovia. Do you think Archie will be okay?"

"Let's hope so dear. Right now, there's not much we can do here. We have to let the police do their job. Let's go home."

Betty piled the kids into the wagon. One by one all but Bob began to cry. "Let's drive around the neighborhoods for a while. Maybe we'll spot Archie," Betty swallowed hard. A frown crossed her face.

Patrick rubbed his eyes with his sleeve. "What if we don't see him? How will he find his way home? He doesn't know where we live."

"Listen, kids, I know you're all unhappy. Let's just hope for the best, okay? I mean, he found us when we left home, right? Maybe he'll find us again."

After an hour aimlessly driving in neighborhoods, the sobs died down. A deafening silence overtook the car. A few times they spotted a large German shepherd, but usually accompanied by someone. There were a few false alarms that raised hopes. That Archie could be gone from their lives began to sink in.

Bob broke the silence. "Mom, let's go home and tell dad. He'll know what to do. He'll find Archie for us." Betty nodded in a resigned way, like she really didn't mean it. They headed back to Cazenovia by the same road they took earlier hoping Archie magically might appear.

When the sad crew arrived home Bob stood on the porch with a broken window screen in his hand. "Betty, what happened to this screen from our bedroom? I saw it flapping in the breeze when I pulled in." The kids piled out of the car. Bob scanned the yard quickly, then looked into the station wagon. Beads of sweat immediately formed on his hairline.

"Where's Archie?" he said, looking at all of them.

Bob junior looked down at his feet, swallowing hard, trying not to cry. The other kids sniffled, remaining silent as though caught committing a crime. Betty collected Lisa from Dooley's lap and said nothing. Finally, Bob summoned the courage to speak.

"Archie's gone. We left him in the house and were on our way to Shopping Town. All of a sudden we looked behind us and saw him running in the road. Mom stopped the car and we took him with us. We thought he'd be okay in the car while we got shoes. Somehow he got out and we can't find him."

"Well, that explains this broken screen. He must have jumped through it then leaped off the porch roof onto the driveway and followed your scent. But how did he get out of the car in the parking lot?"

Dooley looked sheepishly at the ground then started to cry. "I must have left the window down too far in the back seat."

Betty spoke in a hushed tone. "We went to the police. They said bring a picture of him and their patrolmen will be on the lookout. They don't sound optimistic."

Big Bob's eyes widened and he wiped his brow. "We've got to move fast while there's a chance he's still somewhere near Shopping Town." He walked quickly into the house and scoured a drawer in the den until he found a photo of Archie. "This is from a few months back when he was 30 pounds lighter but it will have to do." He taped it to a piece of plain paper and below wrote:

'Lost, June 15, 1958, ARCHIE, Belgian shepherd. 80 pounds. Disappeared from car at Shopping Town parking lot. Contact Bob O'Neill in Cazenovia at Olfield (OL) 5-9182. $50 reward'

Betty looked at the note. "Bob, don't you think that reward is a bit excessive. I know you paid less than that for the dog. Maybe $10 would do. It's a long shot we'll find him anyway."

Bob looked sternly at his wife. "Just leave this to me alright? The dog means a lot to me and to the kids. I know your view. Sometimes you're wrong. Let's just leave it at that." Betty said nothing.

Dooley and Bob stood in silence and looked up to their father. Patrick and the Irish Twins said nothing. Young Bob broke the tense moment. "We want to go with you to the police station. Maybe we'll see Archie on the road."

"Okay, boys, let's go." Big Bob looked at Betty with a furrowed brow. "We'll be back in a few hours. The police can make copies of this notice. We'll tape them to telephone poles up there. Someone must have seen Archie."

They rode quietly in the Gray Ghost to DeWitt. They craned their necks looking for Archie. Bob drove silently, his hands clenched hard on the steering wheel, his eyes scanning the horizon. He wiped his eyes with his sleeve every few minutes. The boys saw he was trying very hard to fight back tears.

"Don't worry, boys. We'll find Archie. He's too important to us to lose him. We haven't seen the best of him yet."

Thirty minutes later they arrived at the police station. Bob explained the situation and a young officer made copies of the paper. "Mr. O'Neill, we'll contact you with good news or bad. You can put these notices on telephone poles within a few miles radius of the shopping center. We have cruisers all over the area so they're on the lookout for him. Just go home. We'll be in touch."

"Dad, what if Archie's hurt?" Dooley looked at his father as the Gray Ghost left DeWitt. "Who will help him?" Tears again welled up in his eyes. His older brother was trying to be strong for both of them but finally emotions got the better of him and tears began streaming down his cheeks.

With his own eyes shining, the man looked over at his sons as he drove toward Cazenovia. It was twilight. "Remember one thing, boys. Archie has in his genes the will to survive. That is the wolf in him. He is very smart. If there is a way for him to find his way home, he will. All we can do is pray he does."

Nightfall arrived and the sky filled with stars as the old truck labored down the country road. Dooley broke the silence. "I wonder where Archie is sleeping tonight," he said. The two Bobs did not reply.

5.   A Miracle

Three long, painful days passed. Bob and Dooley were in no mood to take final exams in school. Dinners took place without conversation. Daily phone calls to the DeWitt police turned up nothing. Before bed all the kids, even the Irish Twins, Maureen and Lisa, who didn't understand the meaning of prayer, knelt by their beds and in their cribs praying for Archie's return.

Late Thursday afternoon Bob and Dooley had returned from their paper route. Spring was turning to summer. Betty, Big Bob and the other three children sat on the porch drinking lemonade that Betty had made to cheer everyone up. Bob had unobtrusively spiked his with Seagram's whiskey. No one spoke. It was as though they were preparing to attend a funeral.

The O'Neill house sat at the base of a long hill. At the crest a gradually moving object, some sort of animal, moved toward them. Big Bob stood, took off his glasses, cleaned them with his handkerchief, and then peered hard at the movement. Whatever it was made its way ever so slowly in their direction. He moved from the porch into the gravel driveway and placed his right hand over his eyebrows to shade the final rays of the afternoon sun. He shook his head slightly.

Betty looked up from her knitting and watched her husband move into the driveway. "Bob, what's wrong? What do you see? "

"I don't know. Maybe my eyes are playing tricks on me. I swear I see something on that hill coming our way but I can't make out what it is. It's not moving very fast."

Betty joined him in the driveway and held her hand above her hand to shade the afternoon sun and squinted. "Too short for a deer. Could be a dog maybe. I can't tell."

Bob and Dooley stopped playing catch and noticed their parents in the driveway focusing on something up the hill. They walked into the yard to get a better look as large maple trees were obstructing their view. As they reached the sidewalk, their arms flew in the air. Their faces showed grins from ear to ear as they erupted into a run up the hill screaming, "Archie, Archie!" A sense of disbelief mixed with hope and fear descended on the entire homestead as the boys' screams permeated the air. Betty grabbed Lisa from the playpen and took Maureen's hand as Patrick followed his father into the yard. One hundred yards ahead of them Bob and Dooley caught up to a gingerly walking Archie who tried in vain to run to greet them.

Tears of joy streamed down Big Bob's cheeks. Patrick and Maureen shrieked. Lisa gurgled a happy baby sound. Big Bob looked skyward and closed his eyes. Betty raised her eyebrows, more out of surprise than anything else.

"Dad, Archie's hurt. He can't walk very good." Bob junior and Dooley hugged their dog as he lay on the Witherall's lawn, exhausted. Tears of happiness gave way to concerns over whether Archie would live.

"Let me help Archie, boys." Big Bob lowered his face to the wolfdog and looked deeply into his eyes that showed the strain of three days of arduous travels. The dog slowly blinked then placed his right paw on Big Bob's shoulder as if to say that his journey was over. "Let me carry Archie home from here," he continued. "We need to take him to Dr. Armstrong to make sure he has no broken bones or other injuries."

Big Bob picked up Archie. "You've shed some pounds, wolfdog. Let's lay him on the porch first so I can take a look. Bob, get a bowl of water and his blanket from the den and lay it out on the porch. Dooley, get a few handfuls of his dog food. Not too much. He might have stomach problems."

Like a wounded soldier coming home, they lay Archie on his blanket as Big Bob surveyed the damage. Archie slowly drank some water from his bowl but refused food. His paws were cut in several places and the top part of his right ear was missing. He had a few deep cuts in his left hind leg and a big claw mark across his nose. An hour later, they laid him on his blanket in the back of the station wagon and the three boys and Big Bob headed to the vet's office.

"He's lucky to be alive, with all these injuries," Dr. Armstrong said, shaking his head. "I can only imagine he got in a few fights with some wild animals. There's a lot of woods between here and DeWitt. Could have been a mother bear, maybe even a wolf, hard to say for certain."

"Not a wolf, for sure, Dr. Armstrong," Dooley interjected. "Archie's part wolf. They wouldn't attack one of their own, would they?"

"They might not know he's part wolf. He's covered in human scents and he's as much shepherd as wolf. Although I have to say, his intelligence and survival instinct undoubtedly helped him stay alive. After I stitch up a few of these wounds, I'm going to send you home with some antibiotics. Archie will need a lot of rest. No running for at least a week."

Big Bob looked at his oldest son. "No paper route for Archie until he's healthy again." Bob junior nodded consent.

"Food wise, introduce small amounts every few hours so his stomach can digest it easily. Start him off with some boiled hamburger and rice mixed with crushed green beans. He needs protein, vitamins and starch. Within four to six weeks he should regain the weight he lost. Most important, just give him a lot of rest."

When they arrived home, Big Bob carried Archie into the den and placed him on his blanket. Everyone stood in a circle around him, just staring, saying nothing. Big Bob broke the silence. "Kids, this is a miracle Archie has returned to us. There are certain times when it's right to say a prayer of thanks. This is one of those times."

So pray they did with the father leading his children in a thankful moment to God for returning their companion. After a moment of silence, Betty broke the pause.

"Okay, kids, we've had a long day. It's time for baths and bed. It's another big day tomorrow. Your teachers are waiting to see you. Just another week and it's summer break."

"But Mom", young Bob interjected, "we should take turns staying with Archie. He's hurt and he needs us."

"Bob, your mom's right. You kids go upstairs and get ready for bed. I'll stay with our friend. He has a lot to tell me about the last three days. I'll let you know tomorrow what he told me."

Dooley looked at Bob and Patrick and nodded. "Guys, it's okay. Dad talks with Archie all the time. We'll find out tomorrow how he made it from DeWitt to here. I bet he got in a big fight with one of those black bears they talk about in social studies."

Patrick looked quietly to his older brothers. "I think ten foxes ganged up on Archie. They're too scared to fight by themselves. That's what I learned from my teacher. Foxes, they like to pick on other animals when they're in a group. Only problem was, they didn't know Archie was part wolf. He's stronger than them." He nodded confidently. His brothers just raised their eyebrows.

"That's good thinking, Patrick," Bob said. "Let's talk about it upstairs."

Summer arrived that night and for the O'Neill kids it was one never to forget. Their prayers had been answered. Archie had returned.

6.   Perilous Journey

T he following night after dinner, Archie limped gingerly to his blanket in the corner of the den. He had moved little that day and did not finish the small amount of food put out for him. Betty let him out briefly to relieve himself. Otherwise, he slept. Big Bob and the three boys surrounded Archie, each staring quietly at the wolfdog. The boys sat cross legged on the aging fake Oriental rug forming a protective wall, gently rubbing Archie's body and head. A small square Bendix television, usually on during the evening hours for an episode of Rawhide or The Rifleman, stood silent. A crooked coat hanger topped with crumpled aluminum foil protruded from the top to replace the antenna severed during a session of den roughhouse football when young Bob, on knees, had tackled Dooley trying to reach a quarter on the couch. The TV had tumbled. It survived minus the antenna.

Archie let out even, shallow breaths, his body quivering from time to time. Bandages covered his legs where Dr. Armstrong had placed thirty stitches. The tip of his bitten-off ear glistened with salve the veterinarian had applied after cauterizing the wound to stem bleeding.

Betty returned from putting the Irish Twins to bed and stood on the edge of the circle, arms crossed. Big Bob glanced at her. She said nothing, her face expressionless. She moved to the rocking chair in the corner of the room and picked up her knitting.

Dooley looked at his brothers and raised his arms in the air as he made a growling sound. "I bet a big bear ate Archie's ear then clawed his nose before Archie could run away." Wide-eyed, Patrick nodded slowly.

Bob junior petted the dog's back. "I think it was a whole pack of raccoons. They got big claws." Patrick remained silent and nodded at this comment also.

Big Bob watched his sons as he poured some whiskey into his coffee then replaced the cap on a flask and took a sip. He placed the mug on the rickety table next to his chair. "Those are good theories, boys. But I can tell you what really happened because Archie and I had a little conversation last night after you went to bed."

Betty pursed her lips, narrowed her brow then shook her head at Bob as she watched him place the flask on the bottom shelf of the end table and close its door until it snapped shut. He leaned back in the threadbare, overstuffed lounge chair. Big Bob ignored Betty's raised eyebrows aimed at him. She rocked gently, needles furiously clacking, knitting a Christmas stocking for a newborn baby girl a friend had just delivered. The three boys immediately turned to face Big Bob eager to learn what Archie had told him.

Bob removed his feet from the ottoman, revealing permanent indentations beneath its thinning leather skin. "Here's what Archie told me, boys. He was confused about being left alone in the car and started to bark because he didn't know if you'd return." He leaned toward his sons, placing his elbows on his knees, gazing deeply into each of their eyes.

"Yeah, I can see that," young Bob interjected, "because we never left him alone in the car before. He was probably real scared."

"That's right. Archie told me he was afraid you would never come back. Then a person approached the car with a cup in their hand, probably water. Maybe the person thought Archie was thirsty on account of it being hot that day. Maybe this person couldn't get the cup in the car through the window so he or she opened the door to put it on the seat. Archie told me he jumped out of the car to go find you."

Betty looked up at her husband and rolled her eyes. Big Bob took a long draw on his coffee.

"How would he know where to go, Daddy?" Patrick said, holding his palms up. "How would he know which store we went to? He didn't know we were buying shoes."

"Good point, Patrick. Archie didn't know where to look because the shopping center was so busy. Even though dogs have an amazing sense of smell, much stronger than people's, Archie told me he couldn't find your scent, so he figured he would try to find our house and he just took off running."

Dooley sat up on his knees getting his father's attention. "But Dad, Archie never left Cazenovia since you and I brought him home at Christmas. How would he know what direction to go?"

"That's the problem Archie faced: he had no idea where to go. He just kept running until he found some woods. I think he got lucky and headed in the general direction of Cazenovia. He told me at the beginning there were cars everywhere with big roads. He told me nothing looked like home. He told me he felt safer in the woods."

"Maybe he liked the woods 'cause he's part wolf, right Dad?" Patrick said confidently.

Upon hearing the word 'wolf', Betty cringed. She dropped a stitch, sighed, unraveled it and started again. A few beads of perspiration appeared on her forehead. She wiped her brow and blew air from her lower lip.

"You're right, Patrick. Archie told me he felt more comfortable in the woods. He also found some streams so he could drink water."

"But what could he eat, Dad?" Dooley questioned. "I mean, we give him his breakfast and dinner and I never saw him eat a squirrel or something wild. He'd get real hungry, right?"

"Archie didn't tell me what he ate, Dooley, just that he found water. He did tell me some scary things he ran into."

The three boys straightened their backs and inched closer to their father, training their eyes on his. "Like what kind of scary things?" young Bob asked.

"Well, Archie said as it became dark he was tired from all the running so he found a place by a stream to curl up and go to sleep. In the middle of the night, some noises caused him to wake up and he smelled other animals nearby. He told me he heard unfamiliar sounds. Then, all of a sudden, strange animals attacked him from all directions, leaping on him and biting him."

"I knew it. Nasty raccoons attacked Archie with their big claws!" young Bob asserted, inching closer to his father.

'It could have been a whole bunch of bad animals," Patrick added, nodding his head up and down confidently as he stroked Archie's back. "They'd need a lot of them to go after Archie. They probably didn't know he was part wolf. Even though Archie's young, he could fight."

Big Bob watched this back and forth opinion. "Boys, I have no idea what those animals were and neither did Archie. All we know is that they meant to hurt Archie, probably have him for dinner. He told me he fought them hard, biting the neck of one and the leg of another. One bit into his ear and tore off the tip. He told me he felt the blood dripping down his neck and he turned real fast and bit the throat of that animal, shaking it from side to side until it stopped fighting and he dropped it right there. It didn't move anymore. Then the rest ran away. Archie took a drink in the stream, feeling real tired, and then walked a while in it thinking the bad animals would not follow him in the water."

Betty looked up and put down her knitting. "Bob, do we really need to tell the boys the bloody details of the dog's adventure? I don't think they need a blow by blow account of what happened."

In unison, the boys looked to their mother. Dooley raised his hands in the air, palms upward. "Mom, we've seen stuff like that on TV. I saw Rin-Tin-Tin bite a wild animal in one episode. We need to know how Archie survived." Betty shook her head and returned to her knitting.

"It's a good thing Archie is strong, right, Dad?" Dooley said, turning back to face his father. "He's big and that helped him fight those bad animals."

"I'm sure it did." Big Bob reached down to the covered shelf, removed the flask and added a little more to his mug before returning the flask to its home. Betty looked at him and cleared her throat, attracting her children's attention. He acknowledged Betty's interruption and nodded benignly to her. "I imagine Archie was much bigger than any one of them but he had to fight however many there were. Those animals probably realized they weren't going to kill Archie so they gave up."

"Then what happened?" Dooley asked raising his eyebrows.

"Archie told me he ran through the dark along the stream until he didn't smell the bad animals any more. Then he fell asleep again until the sun rose. He told me he hurt especially in his legs and his ear. He said he licked the places where the animals bit him but that didn't help much. He was feeling real hungry by now but didn't find anything that might make the pain in his stomach go away."

"How did Archie know he was going toward home?" young Bob interjected.

"He didn't. So he just kept following the stream so he could drink whenever he was thirsty. He must have been heading in the right direction even though he didn't pick up a familiar scent. He just got lucky he picked the right direction."

"How do you think Archie knew to go the right way?" Dooley asked. "I mean, he could have gone toward Chittenango and that's away from Cazenovia."

"Who knows? I just have to believe the god of wolfdogs was looking out for Archie. He just kept following that stream until night fell and he found what he thought was a safe place to curl up and sleep."

Betty bit her tongue. On hearing 'wolfdog', the ball of yarn tumbled from her lap to the floor. "Bob, don't you think the children have heard enough of Archie's journey?"

Young Bob intervened. "Mom, no. We need to hear how Archie got home. We're just getting to the important parts."

"Let's remember, kids," Betty said slowly, "Archie is a shepherd not a wolf. He just got lucky to find his way home." Betty looked at Archie, sleeping, his lips receded, his fangs protruding. She closed her eyes, shook her head and muttered beneath her breath, "Dog, not wolfdog."

The kids all looked at Betty with quizzical expressions. Big Bob took a drink from his mug. They turned to him. "Then what happened, Dad?" Patrick asked, moving closer to his father.

"Well, Archie told me that as the sun peeked through the clouds the next morning, a large animal, bigger than himself, came up to him and bared its teeth."

"What do you think it was?" Patrick asked, eyes widened and focused laser-like on his father.

"It was a bear, I knew it." Dooley declared confidently shaking his head up and down.

Big Bob looked down at his boys. "I don't know what it was. Archie told me he had never seen such a large animal. I imagine it might have been a black bear. They roam in the woods between here and DeWitt. If it was a bear and Archie couldn't escape, it would have killed Archie."

The boys were speechless.

Betty looked up again from her knitting. "Bob, I think we've had enough. We don't want the boys having nightmares."

"Mom, no!" Young Bob stared at his mother. "We're just getting to the important part. We need to know what happened."

Betty returned to her knitting and shook her head.

"Anyway," Big Bob continued, "two things occurred just then."

"What?" the boys blurted in unison, inching closer to their father until they were almost upon him.

At this, Betty put down the knitting needles and, like her children, focused on her husband before turning her gaze to Archie.

"The strange animal lunged at Archie. Before he could escape from it, the animal clawed Archie's nose. That's why Archie has those deep gashes that will be with him the rest of his life. Then, just as Archie was trying to regain his balance from that attack, a huge animal, looking very much like Archie, appeared from nowhere and jumped on the back of the attacker, biting it in the neck. The bad animal howled and ran away."

By now, the boys' faces were a foot from their father's. Patrick grabbed onto Dooley's hand, squeezing it tightly.

"What was it, Dad?" young Bob asked breathlessly. "Who saved Archie?"

Betty's knitting needles stopped clacking. "I think that's enough, Bob. It's getting near bedtime."

"Mom, no!" Three boys shouted in unison. "We need to know what happened."

Pausing for a moment, Bob took another sip from his mug then looked toward the sleeping Archie before focusing on the faces of his three sons. "It was Archie's father, boys. Archie told me he looked at this large animal, much bigger than himself, who spoke to Archie in wolf language."

Mouths agape, the boys remained silent and stunned at this turn of events. Patrick in a soft voice asked, "What did his father say to Archie?"

"He told Archie to go with him to the place where he had met Archie's mother. Then he told Archie to follow the scent from that place to our house. His father told Archie that the two of them would meet again in the after world where all wolves gather to howl at the moon."

The boys stared at their father speechless. Betty shook her head. "Alright, kids, that's enough. Time to go to bed. Archie will be here in the morning. His adventures are over for now."

Dooley ignored his mother and softly said, "So Archie's father took him back to where Archie was born and then Archie found his way back to us?"

"That's right. It took some luck, Archie's strong will to live and the help from the father he had never known. So you can see how special our friend really is. That's why you are the luckiest kids in the world."

The boys gently hugged Archie. "Holy smokes!" Dooley grinned. "Wait 'til I tell the kids in school tomorrow. They're not gonna believe this."

"Yeah," Patrick said in a hushed tone. "I bet their daddies can't talk with their dogs to find out what adventures they have."

Betty shoved her knitting into the basket at her side and rose. "Okay, kids, that's enough excitement for one day. It's time to brush your teeth and go to bed."

The boys rose, kissed their father goodnight and gently petted a sleeping Archie before they filed behind Betty up the stairs. They murmured to each other about the story. "I'm gonna have a good dream about this," Patrick smiled. His brothers tussled his crew cut.

Alone with Archie, Bob drained his coffee as he stared at the dog. He whispered to the dog, "I can only imagine what you truly experienced these past three days."

Archie, aroused by the commotion of the kids heading upstairs, slowly rose to his feet and inched his way to Bob, sitting beside him. Bob gently stroked the dog who arched its back in appreciation. Then Bob closed his eyes and hugged the dog, tears coming that he could not control.

Holding Archie's head in both hands, he looked into the dog's eyes. "Great wolfdog, it is destiny that you survived. You have important things to do for this family. You and I understand this. Now, sleep. Heal yourself and be ready for better days ahead."

7.   Little White Lies

For a solid week the kids followed the veterinarian's orders and made sure Archie stayed around the house and yard. Big Bob checked him daily while changing bandages on Archie's hips and legs, wrapping them in elastic cloth to dissuade Archie from tearing them away. "These wounds are healing okay," he told the three boys. "But there's nothing we can do about the tip of his ear and that gash across his nose. He'll look like that the rest of his life. Kind of like a prizefighter, I guess."

Big Bob pantomimed a few punches in the air. Young Bob and Dooley mimicked him aiming gentle jabs at each other until they grabbed each other's shoulders and tumbled on to the carpet laughing. Big Bob smiled as he counted one, two, three before slapping the carpet and declaring Bob junior the winner. Patrick watched the action, encouraging first one brother, then the other, as he gently petted Archie's head. The dog closed his eyes and arched his neck. "Daddy?" Patrick looked up at his father, who turned away from the rambunctious tussle. "Will Archie be scared of other animals the rest of his life 'cause he got bit a lot?"

The boys rose from their wrestling match, momentarily standing still, watching their father's face.

Big Bob paused a moment then looked at Archie. "I don't think so. Archie's a pretty tough character." He bent down and held Archie's head in his hands as Patrick sat back to watch the exchange. "The wolf in him allowed our friend to deal with some pretty bad hombres on his way home. Archie's a survivor. He'll remember this adventure and learn from it. Who knows? He might face other difficult times. He's not even a year old. In people years, he's about your age, Patrick. He's going to grow, just like you and he'll be fine."

Patrick furrowed his brow. "How come dogs aren't the same age as us?"

"They just age differently than we do. Each one of our years equals seven for them. Archie, if he's lucky, will live to be twelve or thirteen years old. So, if he lives 'til twelve and we multiply that by seven, he'll be about 84. That's as old as Grandpa Hesburgh. When you're a teenager, Archie will be an old man. It's hard to see that now because he's just a puppy. The sad part, I guess, is that all of us, with luck, will outlive our friend. It's never easy to watch dogs grow old much faster than we do. That's why we need to love Archie every day he's with us. "

Patrick's eyes widened and he shook his head in disbelief. "Dad, if I was Archie, I would want to start running now 'cause that's what I like to do best."

"Boys," Bob stressed as he turned to each of his sons, staring directly into their eyes one by one, "Archie can't roam around town on his own like he usually does. We have to wait until he's completely healed."

"Yeah, but what do we tell people?" Dooley asked. "The men who work at all the places Archie visits every day are all asking about him on account of they haven't seen him in a while. And I think Archie will be a lot happier if he can run now. He's been cooped up for a long time."

"You just tell them Archie had a bad adventure. He got hurt and needs a little time to get healed. Dr. Armstrong knows what's best for Archie so we have to listen to him. Archie will be back making his rounds in no time."

"What about the paper route?" Bob asked. "What if we had Archie on a leash? Think he could go with us?"

"Not for a while. We don't want those stitches opening up. He could get infected and we'd have problems. Archie needs to lie low for a while. He'll be fine. Remember when you got the measles and couldn't go to school for a week? No baseball, no paper route, no fun. Remember?"

Young Bob bowed his head, shuffled his feet and reluctantly nodded. "Yeah, I remember."

"Listen, boys, until I say so, only short walks. Put a rope around his neck so he can't take off. Understood?" The boys nodded with their heads and eyes downward.

Big Bob left the house and started up his truck to head to the shop, load a new headstone then lay it at St. James Cemetery.

"It's not fair Archie has to stay inside most of the time," Dooley whispered.

"Yeah, he looks better," Patrick nodded. "He should be able to go where he wants. He looks a lot better than when he came home from the fights with those bad animals."

"This house is like a prison for him," Dooley said. "We need to figure a way to break him loose without mom and dad finding out. It's for Archie's own good. He'll get bored hanging around here with nothing to do."

"You know, guys," Bob cautioned, "We better do what dad says. He's been around dogs more than us. I mean, he talks with Archie. Archie probably tells dad how he feels. Plus, if dad finds out we took Archie someplace against his orders, we could get in big trouble." Patrick and Dooley looked at each other, frowned and nodded.

"I still don't like it," Dooley repeated. "Archie looks plenty good. Right Archie?" And he rustled Archie's head as the dog wagged its tail and hung out his tongue with the large black circle in the center.

Bob put his hands on Dooley's shoulders and looked directly into his eyes. "Just follow orders. We don't need you getting all of us in trouble, okay?" Dooley looked away. Bob shook his shoulders. "Okay?" Bob repeated more firmly.

Dooley scrunched his nose and furrowed his brow before quietly saying, "Okay."

Later in the day, with the boys playing baseball and the Irish Twins napping, Betty sat in the den knitting. Gently moving back and forth in the cherry wood rocker, she glanced at Archie lying on his blanket in the corner asleep. Archie suddenly made little yips and his body shook slightly. His involuntary movements abruptly awakened him and he lifted his head, turning to look at Betty. He tilted his head first right, then left before returning it to the floor. His eyes open, Archie rose from his bed, stretched the length of his body and moved slowly to Betty, sitting in front of her.

She put down her knitting and shook her head. "I don't know what the rest of my family sees in you. I see trouble and expense. Go lie down." And she pointed to the corner. Archie put his tail between his legs and his large ears drooped as he moved slowly back to his blanket.

After another week Archie showed increasing signs of cabin fever. He stalked around the house looking constantly out the windows for the kids. He paced from room to room. Once in the morning and once in the afternoon while the boys were at little league, Betty led him to the front yard. "Go, pee, Archie," she ordered, standing over him like a prison guard. He walked slowly to the side of the garage and relieved himself on some neglected bushes choked with weeds.

Betty noticed the bandage on Archie's left leg was coming loose. She rose from her knitting and approached the dog. She inspected the bandage and wound. "Well, there's no need for you to suffer. I'd better change this." So, she got new bandages and applied them to Archie as he sat patiently and let her repair him. The dog licked her hand as she worked on him and she paused slightly.

Late one afternoon with Big Bob at the shop Betty announced she had to go to the store. "Bob, I'll be back in an hour. Keep an eye on the girls. Dooley, you play with Patrick and make sure he doesn't get into any trouble. I'll be back before you have to do the paper route."

Dooley intercepted his mother at the front door. "Mom, it's okay if Patrick and I take Archie on a rope for a short walk, right? Dad said it was okay so long as he didn't run."

"That's fine, Dooley. But no running. We don't need another trip back to the veterinarian because your dog opened his stitches. Understood?" Dooley nodded while looking at his feet. His left hand remained behind his back where he crossed his index and middle fingers. Patrick stood behind him noticing the hand, tilting his head in confusion and furrowing his brow.

With Betty gone, Dooley wrapped a rope around Archie's neck. The dog jumped about excitedly, placing his paws on Dooley's shoulders and licking his face profusely. Patrick petted Archie's head and looked at his brother. "Archie's ready for a nice walk. Let's go!"

Before they led Archie out the door, Bob grabbed Dooley's arm. "Remember what mom and dad said about Archie. Just keep him on the rope and walk slowly. Right?" Once out of sight from the house, rounding the corner at Liberty Street, the younger brothers approached the open field where they played baseball and manhunt with neighborhood friends.

"Patrick, can you keep a secret?" Dooley turned to his brother.

"What kind of secret?" Patrick replied, his eyes narrowing and a frown forming.

"We need to let Archie run a little. You see him in the house. He's like an animal in a cage. I think he's going crazy 'cause he can't use all his energy. I'm gonna take him off the rope and let him run down here. Maybe he'll see a squirrel or a rabbit. He just needs to run. But it's just our secret, right? Mom and dad, not even Bob, need to know about this."

"Yeah, but you promised mom, dad and Bob you would keep Archie on a rope." Patrick stared at his brother.

Dooley chewed on his tongue a moment, then turned to his brother. "Well, I kind of did. You see, I had my fingers crossed behind my back. So, even if I said one thing, I kind of didn't really say it on account of the crossed fingers. Get it?"

Patrick looked confused as he faced Dooley. Archie strained at the leash as a rabbit scurried across the tree line. "Yeah. I saw when you crossed your fingers when mom was talking to you. But I didn't know what it meant. The other day Father Lynch said in catechism class that lying is saying one thing and doing the opposite. So how come this isn't a lie?"

"Well, there's different kinds of lies. Really bad ones like saying I didn't steal a candy bar from the Five and Ten but actually doing it, that's a black lie, so that's bad. Letting Archie go for a run when I promised to keep him on a rope, that's a white lie. Let's just say it's less bad. Nobody's gonna get hurt and Archie will be happier. What do you think? Secret?"

"I don't want to get in trouble." Patrick looked down at his feet.

"You'll be fine. Just keep your mouth shut. It's our secret. Archie sure isn't going to say anything. Right, Archie?" Dooley looked down at their dog as he ruffled his ears and unhooked the rope from his neck.

Archie took off as if shot from a cannon running in the direction of the rabbit.

The boys remained in the field for half an hour following Archie as he bolted from one edge to another.

"This is the happiest I've seen Archie in weeks," Dooley said proudly.

Patrick raised his eyebrows and shook his head. "We better head back. Bob will be wondering where we went."

They called Archie and the panting dog returned to the boys as he leaped through the tall grass on the edge of the mowed area. Dooley reconnected the rope and they walked home. Once inside, Archie made a beeline for his water bowl in the kitchen where he slurped it for thirty seconds.

Bob sat at the kitchen table feeding the Irish Twins a snack.

"Archie sure is thirsty from just walking, "Bob observed.

"It's getting hotter," Dooley replied.

"What's that red spot on his right leg?" Bob walked over to Archie and saw blood seeping to the surface of the elastic wrap covering the bandage.

"He probably just brushed it up against a tree. It's not dripping or anything. Probably just a scratch from walking. He'll be okay."

Just then, Betty arrived home carrying two grocery bags. "Dooley, you and Bob grab the other bags from the car, please."

She put the bags on the kitchen counter and turned to see Archie. "What on earth happened to him? What's that blood coming through his bandage?"

Dooley looked at Patrick who glanced back staring at his feet, bit his bottom lip and avoided eye contact with his mother. Betty observed this exchange. "Uh, Patrick and I took Archie for a walk like you said we could."

"That's blood." Betty said menacingly to him. "How did that happen if you just walked him slowly?"

Suddenly, Patrick burst into tears. "I don't want to go to hell with the bad angels. Father Lynch said liars go there along with people who steal and do other bad things. Dooley said it was just a white lie, not a black lie. He said it was okay 'cause Archie was just gonna run and be happy."

Betty stamped her foot on the floor, hastily dropped a grocery bag on the counter, and then grabbed Dooley by the scruff of his neck. "Did I not say Archie was to remain on a rope? And what did you do? You deliberately disobeyed me. Bring in the grocery bags then go to your room and wait for your father to come home."

Dooley lowered his head and shuffled out to the car to retrieve a bag. Bob followed in his wake. After they placed the groceries in the kitchen, Dooley headed toward the stairs as he bit on his nails and lower lip alternately.

Bob intercepted him as he started upstairs. "You are in deep doo-doo. Glad I'm not you." The younger brother just shook his head and trudged up the creaky staircase.

Betty approached Patrick, knelt down and hugged him. "You're not going to hell, honey, you're a good boy. You did the right thing by telling the truth. There's no difference between black lies and white lies and don't let Dooley or anyone else tell you there is."

Bob returned to the kitchen. "Mom, want me to do something with Archie's leg?"

"No, your father will be home soon. He'll know what to do. Just make sure Archie remains quiet. Leave him here in the kitchen where I can keep an eye on him so he doesn't drip blood on the rug. You go ahead and do your paper route."

An hour later, Big Bob came home.

"We have a little problem," Betty told her husband pursing her lips. "Dooley and Patrick took the dog for a walk. Apparently, it was more like a run and Dooley lied about it. He's waiting upstairs for you. And him," Betty said pointing to Archie, "I hope he doesn't cost us more to fix him up."

Big Bob inspected Archie, removing the bandage where blood had surfaced. He looked over at Betty who stood by the kitchen sink, her arms crossed. "Fortunately, he didn't do any bad damage. The stitches are still intact. One of them got a little loose and that caused the seepage. No big problem and no need to take him back to Dr. Armstrong. Archie will be just fine." Archie cooperated as Bob applied a new bandage.

Betty turned to her husband as she placed groceries on the shelves. "So, no need to take the dog to the veterinarian?"

"No, he's okay. He's strong and recovering. This is minor."

"Well, it's a relief we don't have to pay more for him now. He's cost us enough as it is. And he's only just as old as Patrick. I can't imagine what he'll cost us if he lives to be old."

Bob glanced sideways at Betty ignoring her comment. "I'm going upstairs to see Dooley."

The boy sat upright on his bed staring at the wall.

"Dooley, you want to tell me what happened today?"

"I just wanted Archie to be able to run. I can tell he's not happy being inside all day. He's probably told you more than anyone because I know you talk to each other."

"Yes, I do understand what Archie wants. He's still a puppy. He's strong and will recover just fine. What's important here is why did you think it was right to lie to mom, Bob and me and then involve Patrick? That's what bothers me more than Archie opening a small wound. Do you understand what you did wrong? Do you understand there are no little lies and big lies? There are only lies."

"Are you gonna hit my fanny with that paddle you got in the Philippines when you were in the war?"

"I don't think that's necessary if you apologize to all of us for lying and promise you won't lie anymore."

"Well, I'm sorry. Is Archie going to be okay? I'd be real sad if I did something to cause him to get hurt worse."

"He'll be fine. Now go down and make peace with your mother."

Dooley approached his mother in the kitchen. "Mom, I'm sorry I lied about running Archie. But you should have seen how happy he was chasing that rabbit. It was like he was smiling!"

"Dooley, what's more important to me than Archie's health is that you understand why there is no alternative to telling the truth. You lied and there is no excuse for that. Your dog doesn't understand what you think he does. He's a dog. They're stupid animals. He'll be fine and eventually get better by staying around the house. You, on the other hand, if you develop a bad habit of lying will be a bad person. And what's worse, you involved your innocent little brother in your conspiracy. Patrick doesn't know how to lie---yet. He thought he was going to hell if he lied. Just tell the truth and think about what your actions mean to others. Plus, what if the dog had broken all his stitches? That's another trip to the vet and another bill to pay, more than you make in a month delivering newspapers. We can't afford that. Just do as we tell you. Now go vacuum the living room and dining room."

As Dooley rounded the corner he bumped into young Bob who had returned from delivering the papers and had eavesdropped on his brother's conversation with their mother.

Bob grabbed his brother's arm and led him to the porch. "Look, Dooley, you're gonna get us all in trouble. What if mom says we can't afford Archie anymore and we have to give him away to somebody who can? Just because dad is crazy about Archie, mom has a lot of say too. If she gets mad enough, Archie might have to go. Something like you did today could cause that to happen. So don't be stupid. Now go do the chores mom told you to do."

Dooley, shoulders drooping, returned into the house and got the vacuum from the hall closet. Just then, Archie approached him and rubbed up against the boy's leg. Dooley bent over and hugged the dog as he whispered into its ear. "I'm sorry, Archie. It's my fault. I won't put you in trouble again. You're gonna live with us forever." Archie licked Dooley's face before returning to his blanket in the den.

Another two weeks passed. Summer in central New York State entered full bloom with temperate days, no humidity, cool, breezy nights and a canine citizen ready to reclaim his playground.

8.   A Dog about Town

Big Bob came in from the garage and sought out Betty in the kitchen. "Betty, Bob wants to take Archie back on the paper route. They want to take him this morning to Little League. What do you think? Is he ready for both of those?"

"Frankly, I don't know and I don't care. The dog stalks the house all day looking out the windows, sniffing at the front door and then barks and goes crazy when one of the boys comes home. Sometimes he wakes the girls from their nap. The sooner he's out of the house the better as far as I'm concerned."

Big Bob raised his eyebrows, ran his fingers through his hair in exasperation and took a deep breath but said nothing. He turned and headed to the utility room near the garage where he found Bob and Dooley gathering their bats and gloves to head to baseball practice. Archie shadowed them.

Dooley turned to his farther. "Well, Dad, is it okay? Can Archie come with us? His bandages are off and he has a lot of energy. Even the top of his ear is crusted over. He doesn't pick at it anymore. We think he's ready."

Archie circled the boys and their father, his tongue hanging out, his tail wagging vigorously, his nose brushing up against the boys' legs.

"Alright, boys. But don't let Archie do anything crazy. I know he looks better but he had some pretty serious injuries. We don't want him getting hurt again." Big Bob bent over Archie and tousled his head and ears. Archie licked his face.

Dooley looked up to his father. "Archie knows something good is happening! He hasn't been this excited since Patrick and I let him loose in the field a week ago." Dooley looked down at his feet to avoid his father's gaze. "Of course," he continued sheepishly, "that wasn't supposed to happen but we know now why it's important to tell the truth." Big Bob nodded approvingly.

"C'mon Archie, let's go play baseball." The boys caressed the dog's head as they collected their equipment and headed out the door, Archie following right on their heels. "See you at lunchtime, Mom," Dooley shouted back into the kitchen, as the Irish Twins played with doll babies on the den floor. Betty waved at them.

Archie pranced like a horse at the starting gate of the Kentucky Derby as he followed the boys to their bikes. He ran behind them along East Lake Road a mile to Lakeside Park where they played ball.

"Archie, you wait over here while we play. We'll be done in a couple of hours." Dooley lingered for a minute gently stroking the dog's head and gave him a hug before turning to face Walt Danks who approached them from first base. The grade school gym teacher headed up the summer baseball league. Archie stretched out in the shade as Walt bent over to pet him.

"Well, look who's back," Danks said as he petted Archie. "Boys, how our favorite dog doing?"

"He's a lot better now, Mr. Danks," Bob replied.

"That's good to hear, Bob. The rumor mill says he had quite the adventure. He looks like he's been in a battle. Wouldn't want to see what the other guys look like."

Archie tilted his head back and forth and licked Danks' hand. As Danks returned to the diamond, last minute stragglers rushed up the field to the backstop, all of them stopping to say, "Hi, Archie," and give him a quick pat on the head.

After a brief nap, Archie rose, yawned and stretched before heading out for his usual downtown walkabout. Passersby pointed at the big dog and called out variations of "Where you been, Archie?" and "Welcome back big fella!" He acknowledged these greetings with a sole bark, then continued on his way. Archie crossed the park in front of St. James Church, then stopped at the back porch of the house on the corner. Sniffing nothing, he barked once. Mandy Talbot often left him a Milk Bone biscuit while Archie waited outside during Sunday mass.

A minute later, Mandy appeared in her customary plaid apron and kerchief holding back her auburn hair. She opened the door and walked out to greet her visitor.

"Hello Archie! Ralph, come here! We have an important visitor." Moments later, Ralph Talbot, the school janitor, wearing blue overalls, appeared in the doorframe.

"Well, I'll be darned. We haven't seen you in several Sundays, Archie. I thought maybe you'd converted to Protestantism. Father Lynch wouldn't like that, you being the altar boys' mascot. Maybe you need a reward for returning to the fold." Ralph smiled at Archie who now sat next to Mandy on the bottom step of their back stairs where she petted him.

Ralph returned with a treat. The dog ate the biscuit, licked Ralph's hand in thanks then headed down Sullivan Street three blocks to downtown.

After a number of stops in the village, Archie sauntered over to Jack Ryan's Funeral Home where he would come with Bob and Dooley that afternoon to collect the papers. No one was in the garage with its chest level wooden bench that ran the length of the building where the delivery boys collected the Syracuse Herald Journal each afternoon and Sunday mornings. So he kept moving past the Brae Loch Inn, crossing East Lake Road and into Lakeland Park, the public swimming place. He took a drink near the concrete pier, swam out about thirty yards, walked back to the sandy entrance, shook off, and then headed past the school and back to the ball field alongside the lake. The boys were just wrapping up morning practice.

Bob and Dooley looked at their wet dog and smiled at each other. Bob stroked Archie's head and looked into his brown eyes. "How ya doin', boy? Looks like you made a little trip down to the lake. Maybe you stopped in some of the places dad saw you visit. You missed your routine, didn't you? Okay, let's go home." Archie wagged his tail like a helicopter blade as he danced around the boys. Looping their baseball gloves through the handle bars, they mounted their bikes and rode home.

As they walked in, Betty held up her hands. "Don't bring him in here like that! I don't want that dog smelling up my furniture and carpets. Find an old towel from the garage and wipe him down before you bring him in." The boys took Archie into the gravel driveway where they dried his thick fur as best they could.

Once inside, Archie lay beneath the kitchen table while the kids devoured cream cheese and jelly sandwiches. Dooley slurped his milk down his chin through a huge mouthful.

"Hey, Mom, Archie's still skinny. Can I give him some of my sandwich? It'll probably will help him grow faster".

She looked at her son sternly. "Dogs shouldn't eat human food. Besides, I learned a thing or two about your dog's little secrets when I went downtown this morning."

Dooley looked at Archie who reclined at his feet. "Sorry, boy, nothing today. Don't blame me."

Betty continued. "Everywhere I went people told me that Archie had paid them a visit. Bucky Bennet told me Archie visits him most mornings and he gives Archie a ham bone, just like today. Then, I went to Aikman's to get a lightbulb and Mr. Evans told me how delighted he was to see his next troop mascot, so he gave him a treat. Then, I had to pick up some cough syrup for Maureen at the drug store. Well, Fred Theobald was gushing about seeing Archie that morning and, of course, he gave him a biscuit."

Bob and Dooley looked at each other with surprised expressions, then focused their attention on Archie. "Wow. Dad told us the other day that on his way to work he noticed Archie heading downtown on his own so he followed him secretly. He said Archie visited those places. We didn't know he did it every day."

As Betty cleared the table she said, "Maybe I should have Archie do all my errands! It would save me time. So, no, Archie doesn't need any of your sandwich. He's not going to starve."

The Irish Twins were clinging to Archie, rubbing his head, whispering "Nice puppy, nice puppy." Archie paid them no heed as he patiently waited to see if something would fall from the table.

"Girls, get away from the dog. He's still wet." She pulled Lisa away from Archie and Maureen followed them into the den.

After lunch, Bob and Dooley played catch in the yard. Archie sat quietly on the porch next to Patrick. The dog's head moved back and forth following the flight of the ball with each throw. His body was alert, head raised high. Bob overthrew Dooley and the ball sailed toward the garage. Suddenly, Archie leaped off the porch and picked up the ball in his mouth.

"Archie, gimme the ball, drop it," Dooley commanded. Archie refused and ran from him like a thief escaping the scene of a crime, stopping at the edge of the yard to look back at the boys.

"Archie, give us the ball, bad boy," Bob yelled, deepening his voice in the hope of commanding respect. Archie still refused.

"Why does he like balls all of a sudden?" Dooley asked Bob, holding his palms skyward. "We don't have a lot of new baseballs. They're expensive. This could be a problem."

"Maybe he thinks they belong to him now," Bob replied, shaking his head.

"Well, it's a bad idea and we have to stop him or he'll take all our balls and then we're in trouble." Dooley gave chase after

Archie. Bob followed. Archie evaded them, running behind Fiedler's house and did not return for half an hour.

The boys dug out another, less desirable baseball. They played catch until it was time to deliver the papers. As they mounted their bikes, Archie appeared right on cue, as if alerted by an internal alarm clock. Bob glared at him. "Archie, bad boy." Archie wagged his tail and held his head high, body erect and ears perked up with tongue hanging down. He walked about the boys excitedly, prancing on all fours, barking happily and nudging them with his nose.

The boys rarely reprimanded Archie so the word 'bad' did nothing to alter his behavior. Bob scratched his head as he looked at Dooley and their dog. "Maybe this is just one of those weird occasions and Archie is testing us. I don't know. We have to make him understand when he does something wrong." His brother nodded.

Bob looked at Archie who sat next to him. "All right, c'mon, let's go. We have work to do."

Having retrieved the papers, they headed out onto their route. "Archie, you haven't done this in almost a month. I wonder if you're gonna remember which houses you deliver." But Archie did recall the routine and performed as though he'd never missed a day.

It helped that many of the customers where Archie delivered saw him coming and gave him a dog biscuit.

Back home, once the papers were delivered, Big Bob and the paper delivery team and Archie piled into the Gray Ghost. A cool evening breeze wafted through the open windows as they headed out Fenner Road to lay a gravestone in Saint James Cemetery.

9.   Ball Obsession

"Archie, quit chewing our baseballs," Young Bob looked down at his dog as he took the animal's big head in his hands and shook it. "I don't get it. All of a sudden he just chases down our balls—one of our good ones—and takes off. And he doesn't give it back to us. What's his problem? He never did this before."

"Yeah," Dooley said frowning at Archie whose tongue hung out as his tail started to move.

Bob shook his head as the corners of his mouth turned down. "Archie's been mostly a good dog. But all of a sudden he starts this crap. And Dr. Armstrong, he says Archie's smart enough that we can train him. You and I got a lot of work to do."

Dooley looked at his brother. "Eventually, he's gotta learn good from bad."

"What if he doesn't change?" Young Bob said, his eyebrows narrowing. "We can't keep buying new baseballs. Each one costs like half a day of what we get delivering papers."

Dooley rubbed his chin. "Remember what Dad said? Archie's still a puppy and all of them like to chew. We need to find something else he can gnaw on that doesn't cost very much. We'll think of something." Dooley placed his hands on his hips and nodded a satisfactory grin.

Bob nodded to his brother. "Dr. Armstrong said a dog's teeth are still forming at his age. Even old tennis balls are better than baseballs, so long as Archie doesn't try to swallow them."

Dooley grabbed Archie's head in both hands and put his face right next to the dog's. "Archie, you have to start learning right from wrong. You get it? If you keep chewing our balls, you're gonna lose your teeth and just eat mush like a real old person." The dog licked Dooley's face. Dooley stood straight up and held his palms upward. "See what I mean? I don't know if he's ever gonna learn. And all we'll have is crummy old chewed-up baseballs."

Bob nodded. "Yeah, we have to teach him." Then he knelt down eye level with Archie. "You're ready to learn, right Archie?" The dog put his nose under Bob's chin and rubbed it side to side.

Over the next few weeks the boys began training Archie.

"Archie," Bob said, "sit and stay." Bob took a good baseball and placed it on the ground in front of Archie. The dog looked at Bob, turned to look at Dooley, then lunged for the ball and headed for the lawn. Dooley was ready for the escape attempt and tackled Archie as he headed for the hill where they ended each paper route. They wrestled and Dooley grabbed the ball from the dog's mouth. He looked at his brother.

BALL OBSESSION

"Well, that didn't work very well," Bob said. "Let's put a ball a few feet from him and try it again."

They made Archie sit and held a baseball in front of his face while repeating 'no' several times. Then they placed it on the ground about five feet in front of him to see how he'd react. Archie stared at the ball and when he made a move toward it, the boys would reprimand him and he sat again. Eventually, he learned that baseballs were not a proper prey.

Realizing they had to make him do what they said, the boys resorted to grabbing Archie firmly across the snout and shaking it, hard enough to make him feel uncomfortable but not so much as to injure him. His tail went between his legs and he slinked on to the porch where they made him lie down in the corner with the gate closed so he could not wander. For a dog who always appeared happiest when on the move, the porch "prison" was a place he hated given his whining as the boys played catch in the yard.

One day they repeated the usual drill. Both boys retreated from the ball, which sat right beneath Archie's head. In unison they said, 'no, no, no'. Archie sat ramrod straight and did not make a move for it. "I think he's starting to get it," Bob said. They then approached him and gave the dog a huge hug, saying "good boy, good boy". Archie stood on his hind legs and placed his paws on Bob's shoulders as he licked the boy's face.

The boys congratulated themselves that they had "cured" Archie. They slapped each other on the back and declared victory. Bob faced Dooley. "It was a lot of effort but Archie knows now that baseballs are off limits. That's a good thing."

One day, Dooley chased an errant throw from Bob that went behind the garage. He noticed that the weed infested space near a column of dying arbor vitae had become a tennis ball graveyard. He scratched his head as he called his brother to come over. They gazed on a vast pile of perhaps seventy green tennis balls in various stages of being chewed to their core. "I wonder where they all came from," Dooley said as he turned to his brother.

"Beat's me," Bob said.

The boys stared at the pile. Finally, Bob spoke. "We should check out the college tennis courts. Where else would anyone use this many tennis balls?" The courts were just three blocks away.

A few days later, after they had delivered the papers, they left Archie on the porch and went down to the college tennis courts and waited to see what might happen. Lo and behold, after settling in behind some hedges across the street from the courts, Archie comes sauntering down the street.

The boys moved behind a big Buick Special. Thirty yards away, they watched as Archie lay behind some tall bushes bordering the courts. The boys heard a girl's shriek and watched a misguided ball fly from the court. They watched Archie's head trace the arc of the ball as it bounced on the sidewalk. It headed toward Liberty Street. Archie bolted from a prone position and caught the ball in midair off a bounce then made a beeline for home.

"Archie, stop!" Dooley and Bob yelled as he sped by them, paying no heed to their command. "C'mon, Bob, let's get him." As they turned to follow Archie, they saw a young co-ed in a turquoise tennis skirt walk around the hedges and scratch her head in disbelief at the disappearance of her ball.

Betty soon received a call from Irene Burke, the assistant to Rhea Eckel, the Cazenovia College President for whom Betty did occasional secretarial work.

"Betty, it's Irene. How are you doing?"

"Oh fine, Irene. Does Mrs. Eckel need some extra help this week?"

"No. not really. She asked me to call you about tennis balls."

"Come again, Irene. Tennis balls?"

"Yes, she has an unusual request."

"Oh, I see," Betty replied awkwardly. "But what does that have to do with tennis balls?"

"Well," Irene continued, "it seems our tennis coach, Ed English, saw a dog looking like Archie lying behind the tennis courts during practice. We appear to be losing a lot of balls. He suspects Archie is taking them. Can you check with your kids to see if he's doing that and stop him? Mrs. Eckel says the college doesn't have a budget for unlimited balls."

"I'll look into this right away and if Archie is the culprit he has stolen his last tennis ball. In fact, if he's guilty, the boys will use their paper route money to replace the balls he stole."

"No, Betty, that's okay. It's not a federal offense. It's tennis balls. We'll handle it. If it is Archie, just have the boys stop him. I know he's a good dog. He's apparently ambitious in the wrong way. He delivers Mrs. Eckel's paper just fine so I'm sure he's smart and can learn to stop being a ball thief. Just let us know how you make out."

At dinner that night, Betty raised the subject with Bob and Dooley. "Boys, I had a call from Cazenovia College today. Apparently, your dog has been stealing tennis balls from the college. You're responsible for him. I don't want any problems. I told you before. Archie is on probation."

The boys looked at each other with furrowed brows. Bob looked Betty in the eye. "Yeah, we'll check it out, Mom." Bob turned his head away from Betty, looked at Dooley and raised his eyebrows and bulged his eyes signaling for Dooley to remain silent. "If Archie is stealing any, we'll make sure he stops."

Betty let out an exasperated breath. "Sometimes, this dog is more trouble than he's worth. Just make sure he doesn't cause more problems. I don't want to get calls from anyone in town complaining about him. Understand?"

The boys sheepishly nodded then took Archie out to the front porch. They sat with him between them. Bob grabbed Archie's nose, forcing the dog to look directly into his eyes.

"Archie, if you want to stay with us, you have to stop stealing these." Bob held a well-chewed tennis ball at the end of Archie's nose. "This means no!" Bob rubbed the ball along Archie's snout as he continued to say 'no, no, no'. Archie rolled over putting his paws near his face.

Over the next few days, the boys monitored Archie closely. Whenever he tried to sneak down Union Street toward the college, they stopped him, held a tennis ball to his nose and shouted 'no' at him. Eventually, they broke Archie of his robber habits. About the time Archie ceased stealing tennis balls he became enamored with footballs.

With fall in full bloom, footballs replaced baseballs. Bob and Dooley played catch for hours. A misguided throw before a vigilant Archie generally resulted in a chase. Ultimately, Archie chewed off the leather exterior of the football exposing its pigskin.

"Archie, this is no!" Dooley held a football beneath Archie's nose, half the outer skin missing. The dog looked up at the boy and licked his face. Dooley shook his head. "Bob, we got a problem, here. Archie understood tennis balls and baseballs. He just refuses to understand that footballs are off limits."

The boys stopped buying good footballs and resorted to the cheap variety. They never had a complete football. Usually only 20% of the exterior remained. Fortunately, the balls remained serviceable as Archie just chewed the exterior and did not puncture them.

Rocks became Archie's Achilles heel. While he caught baseballs and footballs (he never dominated basketballs as they were too big) rocks began to wear down his teeth. The boys fed this practice as they wanted to preserve their footballs and saw rocks as a no-cost alternative. They started throwing small rocks Archie's way and he caught them.

Big Bob saw this. "Boys, we can't do that. Archie's going to lose all his teeth. Remember what Dr. Armstrong said. Archie has to chew soft things. Rocks will crack his teeth and create gum problems. Let me find a solution. Just stop giving rocks to him."

A week later, Big Bob returned from the high school. Over his shoulder he carried a yellow mesh bag full of footballs.

"Dad, what do you have there?" Bob junior asked.

"Boys, I went to see Walt Danks. He said every football season they need to buy new balls. I asked him what he did with the old ones and he said they usually just throw them out. So, I told him I have a better use."

Dooley put his left arm around Archie's back. The dog was almost full grown.

"Archie," Dooley looked in the dog's eyes. "We have something good for you. No more rocks. Look at this." He took a ball from the mesh bag.

The 130-pound wolf-dog looked back at the boy and took the football in his mouth. The footballs lasted a long time. The O'Neill boys stopped offering Archie rocks and he didn't chew them anymore. Footballs became a lifelong obsession for Archie.

10.   Thanksgiving Feast

Dooley and Bob sat in the den watching *The Rifleman.* "Boys, when your show's over, set the dining room table with grandma's good china and the silverware from the fancy wooden box. We want everything to be ready for tomorrow. Grandpa and Grandma are coming. Everything has to be perfect for them. I'm so excited. It's going to be a wonderful day!"

"Okay, mom," they responded in unison without taking their eyes off of Chuck Connors dispatching another bad hombre who'd done him wrong.

Archie lay in the doorway connecting the den with the kitchen, his eyes moving methodically across the room, watching the commotion as Bob and Dooley broke the bread into ice cube-sized pieces while Betty cooked a concoction of broth and herbs on the stove to blend with it. Bob opened two tubes of Purnell's country sausage, handing Dooley one.

"This stuff feels really gross," Dooley grinned as sausage squished between his fingers, "like monster brains!"

As the smell of sausage permeated the kitchen, Archie rose and moved next to the boys lifting his nose to the table's level. Dooley shook his hands toward the pile of bread and remnants hit the floor. Archie scarfed them up as Betty monitored the boys' progress.

"Boys, don't let Archie eat that raw sausage. It's not good for a dog's stomach." Then she muttered under her breath, "Not that he'd know the difference."

The boys kneaded the bread and sausage amalgam, forming baseball-sized spheres while Betty greased the turkey's cavity with oleo. Archie's eyes never strayed from the bird. Saliva dripped from his muzzle. The boys loaded the bird, Betty sewed the legs together and into the oven it went.

"Mr. Turkey's all set," she smiled. "I do love that smell in the morning. Now, Bob, you and Dooley get Patrick. Take the Hoover and some furniture polish and clean the living room, dining room and den. We want the house to look just right for Grandma and Grandpa."

Archie, meanwhile, quietly walked to the oven and stared blankly at the solid door where the sacrificial bird lay inside. "I think Archie likes Mr. Turkey, Mom," Bob laughed.

Betty grabbed Archie by the scruff of his neck, steering him away from the oven. She leaned close to his face. "Archie, Mr. Turkey is not yours. If you're a good dog, we'll give you some leftovers, just behave." Archie sat obediently and looked at Betty. He tilted his head first right, then left, his nose seeking the scent of Mr. Turkey.

Bob checked the clock then barked orders like a drill sergeant. "Patrick, you put all the toys in the toy box. Dooley, you run the vacuum. I'll polish the tables."

The three boys moved like a SWAT team through the rooms to make them presentable. The Irish Twins played with their infant brother, Timmer, an addition to the clan born eight months earlier on St. Patrick's Day. Betty emerged from the kitchen and walked about the house examining everything, the boys trailing in her wake as they eyed the clock and television simultaneously. *Have Gun, Will Travel* began in ten minutes. Betty gave the thumbs up. Dooley moved to the toy box to locate his cowboy hat, holster and pistol. "Hurry up, guys. It's starting in a few minutes."

"Yeah, I wonder who Paladin will get tonight," Bob replied. Archie looked wistfully in the direction of the stove before following the boys into the den.

Big Bob arrived home from the shop, stone dust covering his clothes. Archie rose quickly and approached his master who vigorously rubbed the dog's head. "Great wolfdog, are you ready for our big feast?" Archie pawed Bob's leg as Betty came into the entryway from the kitchen.

"Well, everything's all set. I'll turn on the oven at nine. The boys set the table and cleaned the downstairs. It's just going to be perfect. Tomorrow, when we wake up the whole house will smell wonderful."

Bob smiled at Betty then removed his boots and walked into the den. "Hi boys, how's it going with our friend, Paladin, tonight?"

"Hey, Dad," young Bob replied without moving his eyes from the Bendix. Dooley and Patrick waved at their father while staring intently at the TV. "Yeah, Paladin's good. He's just about to catch this bad guy who robbed a bank."

"That guy has no chance," Dooley blurted out. Patrick, sitting cross-legged on the old oriental nodded silently.

Thanksgiving morning arrived with the distinctive scent permeating the house. "Kids, Mr. Turkey is coming." Betty smiled as breakfast spoons, metronome-like, scooped Cheerios into eager mouths. Archie, as usual, reclined beneath the kitchen table awaiting misguided pieces that might hit the floor. Big Bob, in white tee shirt and flowered boxers, drank black coffee and smoked a Salem. "It'll be a perfect Thanksgiving, kids. And wait 'til grandma sees our new dishwasher. She never had one like that."

"Yeah, Mom," Dooley said through a mouthful of Cheerios, "Everybody's gonna be happy today."

"We have a lot to be thankful for this year, Dooley. Grandma and grandpa will be happy to share this day with us." She sighed contentedly looking into the dining room as sunlight reflected off the silverware. The perfectly set table awaited the arrival of Mr. Turkey as its centerpiece.

At noon, Betty's parents arrived. Grandpa Theo removed his felt fedora and walked about the room hugging Betty and the girls, and shaking hands with his grandsons and Big Bob. He wore a gray pinstriped suit, starched white shirt and a pumpkin colored tie. Grandma Bess displayed a festive hat cocked to one side with a long plume sticking out the back. She sat down and removed a wrinkle from her flowered dress accented by a light orange sweater.

Big Bob wore a slate blue suit with a solid red tie, the same outfit he used for mass each Sunday. Betty modeled a red dress with blue piping, her favorite colors. The three older boys wore their Sunday best: ironed collared shirts, khaki pants with a firm crease, dark socks and shoes polished so well they could almost see their reflection in them. The Irish Twins wore matching frilly dresses. Timmer sported a shirt with a pilgrim on the front and brown corduroys.

Archie greeted Betty's parents like long lost friends. Grandpa Theo vigorously rubbed Archie's ears and Grandma Bess petted his back with her gray gloved hand.

"How old is Archie now?" her father asked Betty.

"He's four, Dad," she replied with taut lips. "Sometimes it seems like I have seven children, not six."

Her father nodded. "Still got a lot of puppy in you, huh, Archie?" The dog held out his paw toward Theo.

Before dinner on an unseasonably warm day, the adults enjoyed highballs on the porch as Bob and Dooley played football in the yard. Patrick and the Irish Twins occupied themselves with Timmer in the playpen nearby. Betty shouted into the yard, "Boys, be careful you don't get those good clothes dirty."

They inspected themselves and shouted back, "We'll be careful, Mom."

Big Bob nursed his third Seagram's and Seven. Betty discreetly took him aside. "Bob, is it necessary to drink so much? It's not even three o'clock."

"I'm fine. Just make sure your parents are happy."

Betty turned off the oven and removed Mr. Turkey encased in his silver armor. She placed the bird on the kitchen counter to cool. Betty turned to her husband. "You can cut Mr. Turkey in thirty minutes then we'll sit down. "

Twenty minutes later, Betty excused herself from the porch to check on her signature feast. She entered the kitchen and saw Archie stretched out on the floor breathing heavily. His stomach looked like he had swallowed a beach ball.

Fragments of turkey covered the floor with gravy drippings splattered over the mustard colored cabinets like a crime scene. Evidence from the vicious slaughter was strewn in all directions. The victim's carcass lay on the middle of the floor. Shredded pieces of aluminum foil littered the area over a six-foot radius. A mangled drumstick leaned against the new dishwasher. Clumps of sausage dressing clung to the legs of metal chairs. Only the side dishes, covered bowls of mashed potatoes, green beans and squash, placed in the middle of a crowded Formica kitchen table, were spared from the carnage.

Betty stumbled back, leaning against the doorjamb for support, gasping for breath, unable to let out any sound. Finally, she shrieked a blood-curdling cry, "Boooobbbbb!"

Big Bob rumbled into the house with parents-in-law trailing. Betty's hands pushed against her temples, face red, tears streaming down her cheeks, saying nothing, just heaving deep breaths.

Bess hurried to Betty, enveloping her daughter, caressing Betty's head and whispering in her ear. Surveying the scene, she spoke in a measured tone. "Oh my goodness, I've never seen anything like this. What has that dog done?" She shook her head and rubbed Betty's shoulder.

"Oh, well. Worse things have happened. But, my, what a mess." Grandpa Theo looked at his distraught daughter. His wife and daughter looked at him with disagreement in their faces. Theo turned to his son-in-law who stared at the floor with his mouth agape. Archie just lay amid a thin lake of gravy. Theo removed his white cloth handkerchief and cleaned his wire rim glasses. "So, what's your plan Bob?"

Big Bob rubbed his eyes. Beads of sweat appeared on his hairline. His shoulders slumped. Everyone turned to look at him. He said nothing, just continued staring at the scene as he tried to compose himself from a whiskey induced state. After what lasted thirty seconds but seemed more like thirty minutes, he said, "Let me get Archie outside then we'll figure out dinner." He grabbed Archie by the scruff of his neck and the dog rose laboriously to his feet. Archie moved slowly, his stomach distended. Bob led him outside slowly to prevent another disaster, Archie vomiting on the kitchen floor. Archie plopped down near the hedges and instantly fell asleep.

The kids began piling in from the porch and yard with young Bob holding Timmer. They passed their father in the hallway leading Archie outside. "Dad, why are you taking Archie outside?" Patrick asked. Bob said nothing, just continued through the front door with a dog they saw who was somehow out of sorts.

Once inside, their eyes widened and became frowns as they saw the adults surrounding a huge mess. Maureen and Lisa looked at each other and pointed to the floor.

Patrick turned to Dooley and whispered, "What happened to Mr. Turkey? Did he explode out of the oven?"

Dooley shook his head. "This isn't good. You saw dad leading Archie outside. I'm pretty sure he ate Mr. Turkey. Mom said he's already on pro-bra-tion."

Patrick frowned. "What's that mean?"

"That means mom might have Archie leave." Dooley turned to his older brother and whispered, "Archie's in big trouble, Bob. What are we gonna do?" Bob raised his eyebrows and shook his head as he stared at his mother waiting for her to say something. Betty wiped her eyes with a tissue, pushed back her hair from her face and took a deep breath.

Big Bob returned to the kitchen. He took Timmer from young Bob and handed him to Grandma Bess. He instructed Bob and Dooley to clean up the mess. Betty stood near the sink, her face red as a tomato. She turned to her parents. "Mom, Dad, I'm sorry you had to experience this. You deserve better. I wanted this to be a special day for all of us. Now, it's all gone wrong."

Theo pursed his lips. "Betty, it's not your fault. You did everything you could."

Stiffening her chin, her eyes narrowing, Betty addressed her husband. "Bob, what are you going to do with that damn dog? He has ruined everything."

"Betty, we just had a small setback. Archie's not himself."

"Not himself," Betty interrupted, "Your wolfdog just ate our Thanksgiving dinner. He weighs more than me. He's what? Twenty eight years old in people years? He just devoured a meal for eight. He's a menace. What don't you understand?"

Bob squirmed as he stood. He wrung his hands together. The sweating around his temples became more pronounced. He arched his neck seeking to stimulate oxygen to his addled brain. "Betty, okay, he did something out of character. He's never done this before and I know he won't do it again. We'll be fine. He needs a little training. We can make everything right."

Betty threw her hands in the air. "No, no, no! Everything will not be alright! I have had it! I don't like your damn dog. I never wanted your damn dog! He has ruined my day! I want him gone! Give him to the Weavers! I saw Agnes at the store the other day. They have a big farm. They want a large dog to ward off foxes. Maybe Archie could do something productive! Instead of eating Mr. Turkey he could kill foxes! Call Joe Weaver! Call him now! I want the damn dog gone!"

Big Bob appeared like a prizefighter backed into a corner with no idea how to parry the body shots he was taking in front of a crowd of spectators. His eyes widened. His mouth remained open but no words came forth. Timmer began to cry. Then, in a chain reaction, the Irish twins started to cry, joined by Patrick. Theo and Bess looked at Bob with raised eyebrows then down at their feet.

Bob chewed on his tongue and flexed his fingers. He stood silent. Betty and his in-laws stared at him as though this entire tragedy was all his fault.

Through sniffles, Patrick saved him from further scrutiny as he stepped toward his mother. "Archie's sorry, Mom. Can't he just stay on pro-bra-tion?"

Betty looked down at Patrick, raised her eyebrows, then shook her head. "Patrick, I don't think you know what that means. But even if you did, I have reached the end of my patience with that animal. Probation is over. Archie must go!"

Dooley, teary-eyed, put his arm around Patrick's shoulders and stepped between his parents. Young Bob stood with a handful of greasy paper towels nearby, his eyes transfixed on his mother.

"Mom," Dooley implored, staring into Betty's eyes, "Patrick's right. Archie's sorry. He did something bad. We know that. But that doesn't mean he's a bad dog. He's our best friend. He's the whole town's best friend. Everybody on the paper route, the people in the stores he visits, the kids at school, our baseball coaches, even Father Casey, and he's related to God. They all love Archie. We gotta keep him. We can't send him to the Weavers. They don't know Archie. He'd be lonely without us and we'd be sad without him. You have to give Archie another chance!"

All the children stepped forward, nodding in unison. Patrick approached his mother and took her hand.

"Mom," he said, "Archie's like another brother. He looks out for us. We love him. We know he ate Mr. Turkey, but that wasn't the dog Archie, that was the wolf Archie. We can make him be more like a dog. Dooley is right. We have to give Archie another chance".

Betty looked at her children and crossed her arms, staring stonily at them. She took a deep breath, exhaled and rubbed her throbbing temples. She sat at the kitchen table and said nothing for thirty seconds. Finally, she looked at them and spoke in a slow, measured tone.

"Kids, I appreciate that you love Archie. I know what he means to you. I do." She paused for ten seconds and placed her hands together on her lap. "I'm sure Archie loves you too. All he wants is to be with you." Again she paused and took a deep breath as she looked at her parents as though to invite them to say something, which they did not. "But Archie has to change. He can't just do whatever he wants whenever he wants. There are rules. Do you understand?"

The kids and even Big Bob, caught in the emotion of the moment, nodded. The cries and sniffles subsided quickly.

"You know, Mom," young Bob said, "We trained Archie to not steal tennis balls so I'm sure we can train him not to eat turkeys."

Betty straightened out a crease in her dress and looked at her parents as if to invite their counsel. They returned blank stares. She relaxed her shoulders as she looked into her children's faces. "All right," she said in a resigned manner. "We'll give Archie one more chance. But one more bad thing and I call Joe Weaver. Understood?"

They all nodded, looking at each other and smiling thin smiles like the criminal who escapes the noose and lives another day.

Betty composed herself. "Well, we're all here and Thanksgiving has to go on. I think I have some chicken and leftover pot roast in the Frigidaire." She fired up the fryer and within ninety minutes dinner was ready.

After dessert, the three older boys cleared the table and loaded the dishwasher. Betty, her parents and the three younger children retreated to the living room. Betty sat in the middle of her brown and yellow flowered couch surrounded by the kids who looked at picture books their grandparents had brought about the first Thanksgiving feast.

Grandpa Theo moved to the large rocker and lit the pipe he reserved for special occasions. Grandma Bess settled comfortably into the overstuffed leather armchair with matching ottoman. Big Bob took his coffee outside to check on the perpetrator. He found Archie where he had left him three hours earlier.

"Great wolfdog," Bob said as he knelt over the dog and looked into Archie's glazed eyes, "You must learn some human customs. I know you understand me. I realize this from the first time we met. You can be part of our great feasts but you cannot eat our feast. Do you understand me?" Archie belched loudly, then he returned to sleeping.

Big Bob paused for a moment, unsure whether he was communicating with Archie who did not seem alert at all. Archie opened his eyes momentarily, then closed them. Bob reflected for a second then whispered to Archie. "Am I getting through to you, wolfdog? Do you understand me? We need to agree on what you can do." For a fleeting moment, he wondered if his awkward communication with Betty was more than the disagreement they had over Archie.

Archie's eyes appeared as heavy as his stomach. He made little movement. The only testament to his understanding of Bob's guidance was that never again did he repeat the Thanksgiving massacre.

11. Road Trip

Big Bob sat in the office at his shop facing an ancient roll-top desk with its multiple shelves and cubby-holes stuffed with gravestone drawings. Stone dust covered everything. Piles of drawings and other papers lay on the floor held in place by a piece of granite or marble. He sighed then reached in the center shelf and unrolled the ultra-thin paper with charcoal markings he had prepared for Jimmy Gibson's marker.

He leaned back in the old swivel rocker that creaked as he took a long draw on the hot black coffee. Dooley, who had come with his father this Saturday morning to clean up the dust on the sand blasting floor, stuck his head in the office doorway. "What are you looking at, Dad?"

"This drawing I did for a lady in Ohio. It's one of the hardest I ever had to make."

"How come?"

"Well, it's the circumstances I guess. This lady had a son, Jimmy. About your age. He loved baseball and playing the guitar. Around Thanksgiving, he got run over by a truck while riding his bike. Horrible accident. His mom was crying on the phone as she told me what happened. She wants a special stone laid at his grave.

It kind of hit me extra hard." Bob put the drawing on his desk, removed his glasses, closed his eyes and rubbed his temples.

Dooley moved to his father and placed his hand on Bob's shoulder. "But I bet these stones you make let the people feel a little happier, right Dad?"

"I suppose so, Dooley." Bob withdrew the handkerchief from his overall's front pocket and cleaned his glasses before putting them on and smiling at his son. He picked up the drawing as they both looked at it.

"I think his parents will like that, Dad. When do you have to lay it on his grave?"

"In a few weeks. Actually on January 17, the day Jimmy would have turned eleven. Well, let's head home. I'll go to work on this Monday."

Two days later Bob returned to the shop to finish the job. He put on his extra thick overalls, then donned the clear plastic mask to cover his face before cranking up the sandblasting machine. Pulling the wand's lever, a stream of high pressured sand carved indentations into Vermont granite like a hot knife through butter. Enveloped in a small room with thick plastic foot-wide strips to contain most of the stone dust, he looked at the four-foot high gray marker sitting atop a ten inch base. He had taken his charcoal drawing, transferred it to half inch thick rubber cemented on one side, and applied it to the stone. By blasting around the carved rubber portraying the drawing, the sand dug into the granite while bouncing off the rubber to create the effect Bob wanted.

He finished the diagram then blasted around the rubber letters and numbers that read: Jimmy Gibson, January 17, 1951-November 27, 1961. He focused on the second date for a moment. That had been Thanksgiving Day. He felt a shiver run down his spine. On that day, the O'Neill's had lost a turkey. Jimmy's family had lost their son.

He cut the compressor's motor, lifted his protective mask, peeled off the rubber strips with a chisel and set of tongs designed for the job, then stood back as the dust cleared. He circled the monument, leaving footprints as if he'd walked through inches of new-fallen snow. He lit a Salem then examined each part of the marker for fifteen minutes. A lump emerged in his throat. Most of the people's names he carved in monuments had celebrated long lives, veterans, parents who lived long enough to attend weddings, college graduations and bounce grandchildren on their knees, husbands and wives, laid to rest by each other after fifty years of marriage. Bob wiped his eyes, closed down the shop and headed home.

Returning home, he found the house quieter than usual, since Bob, Dooley, and Archie were delivering papers, leaving only

Patrick, Timmer, and the Irish twins in the den playing with toys. Betty was in the kitchen preparing dinner. She did not look up when he entered.

"I have to take a trip to Ohio. Remember, I told you about that young boy who was killed in a bike accident?"

"Oh, yes, I remember. Just ten or eleven, right?"

"Yes, their only child, Jimmy. Poor guy. Died on Thanksgiving Day. All he ever wanted was to play center field for the Indians and start a rock and roll band. "

"It's a horrible thing to lose a child, especially one so young. When do you go?" Betty shook her head as she stirred spaghetti.

"A couple of weeks. I was thinking I'd take Archie with me. I could use the company. Maybe a change of scenery would do him good. What do you think?"

She pursed her lips. "I'm fine with it. Do what you think's best."

Bob bit his tongue. Over the recent weeks their conversations had been brief and transactional, nothing heartfelt or certainly not humorous. It was as though they had forgotten how to laugh together. More often than not, Bob found himself in the mornings on the couch in the den, a bottle of Seagram's almost gone and the test pattern on the TV emitting a low, constant drone.

Young Bob and Dooley looked at each other with raised eyebrows when Bob mentioned over dinner the trip with Archie. They both fidgeted in their seats as they put down their forks. Dooley addressed his father. "Yeah, well, do you think that's such a good idea, Dad? I mean, Archie's never been outside Cazenovia except, of course, for when he got lost in the woods. Maybe he'd be confused. He depends on Bob and me, you know?"

"I'll think he'll be okay. A change of scenery might do him good."

Dooley turned to his mother. "What do you think, Mom?"

Betty cleaned the corners of her mouth with her paper napkin, before replacing it on her lap. "I think it's fine. Your father could use the company. It's a long trip to Ohio."

The boys looked at Archie lying between them on the floor. Young Bob spoke next. "Mom, we know what you said at Thanksgiving about Archie going away if he was bad again. I mean, he's been pretty good the last month, right? He's not going to Ohio for permanent, is he?"

"No," Betty said, her eyes fixed on her plate, "but Archie is still on probation." She looked up at her two older sons. "Yes, he's behaved better since that awful Thanksgiving Day. If he continues to be good, he can stay. But one more episode like before and he is gone. Understood?"

The older boys nodded. Patrick used his shirt sleeve to wipe off spaghetti sauce that covered the lower half of his face. Betty looked at him and cleared her throat as Patrick quickly took a paper napkin to finish the job. "Hey, Archie," Patrick said, grinning, "Looks like you're taking your first trip from home. What do you think, boy?" At the sound of his name, Archie's ears stood erect. He raised his head and approached Patrick, stuck out his tongue and wagged his tail.

Two weeks later, amid the usual mid-January snowstorm that engulfed Cazenovia, Big Bob loaded the 1959 heavy-duty Dodge truck with the winch in the back. "Big Bertha," as he called it, had succeeded the Gray Ghost, which had died an unceremonious death. Early that morning he had gone to the shop, backed in Bertha, applied heavy-duty cloth strips around the marker, maneuvered the winch into position then lifted the stone onto the truck's bed. He covered it with canvas, secured the gravestone with heavy ropes, then drove home.

"Big Bertha and I are ready," he announced after breakfast. "Jimmy's stone is loaded on the back. Archie and I have a reservation at the Holiday Inn outside Ashtabula. Probably going to take us a good seven hours to make it there. We see the Gibsons tomorrow morning at ten."

"We have a bag with Archie's food, Dad, enough for a few days. We put it on the floor of the truck. We put an old blanket in there too, in case Archie gets cold."

"That's great, boys. I think he'll be fine. This'll be a good adventure for our young friend."

The family gathered on the porch as Big Bob placed his overnight bag on the passenger side floor of the truck. "Archie, you ready for our big adventure?" The boys and the Irish twins took turns hugging Archie who perked his ears then approached the door. Betty held Timmer. She gave a cursory wave and headed inside. The dog leaped into the cab, Bob cranked up the engine and away they went.

Heading out of Cazenovia toward the New York State Thruway, WNDR played Sinatra's "Ain't She Sweet" as Archie stretched out on the seat, his head resting comfortably on Bob's thigh. He massaged the dog's head. "Great wolfdog, this is the first time in a long while that we are alone. Do you remember when we first met?" Archie lifted his head, turning his large brown eyes toward his master. He licked Bob's hand then rubbed his head against Bob's leg. The snow subsided as they approached Buffalo heading southwest toward Erie in the gathering dusk.

Outside Erie, Bob spotted a man standing next to a car with no lights waving his hands. He pulled over in a deserted, unlit rest area generally reserved for large trucks. Cutting the motor, he lowered his window halfway to give Archie some fresh air. He left the cabin lights lit and got out. "Archie, you stay there." The dog sat up and looked out the back window as Bob approached the man whose head was covered by a hooded sweatshirt beneath a torn parka.

"What seems to be the problem, friend?"

"No problem at all, man, so long as you fork over all your cash." The disheveled man threw back the hood and withdrew a large Bowie knife from inside his coat. His eyes bulged and sweat appeared on his brow despite the cold weather. A scraggly beard covered his lower face. He pointed the knife at Bob and waved the weapon in circles.

Bob raised his hands and inched back slowly toward the truck. Moving forward, the man blurted out, "Hold it there, buddy, you ain't going nowhere 'til I get me some cash. Just hand it over and we won't have no problem." Archie began to growl, drawing the would-be outlaw's attention. "Then, you and Rin Tin Tin there, can just keep moving. Just cough up the damn cash! Get it?"

"Look, mister, I don't want any trouble. I'm just a simple tradesman on my way to deliver a gravestone. I'm not rich. I thought you were in trouble so I stopped. Why don't we just go our separate ways? You got problems and I can't help you."

"Oh, yeah, you're gonna help me." The robber inched closer to Bob, brandishing the large knife. "I need cash and I'm sure you got some. So just fork it over and get the hell out of here."

Archie stuck his snout through the driver's window, his growls increasingly guttural. He scratched at the door feverishly with both front paws. He whined in a high pitch and paced back and forth like a caged lion. He clawed at the partially open window standing on his hind legs. His breathing became heavier as the noise reached a feverish pitch.

"Tell your damn dog to shut up."

"He senses I'm in trouble. He's not going to stop barking until he thinks I'm safe."

"Well, that ain't happening 'til you give me some dough. Come on, you're wasting time. Just gimme the damn cash, goddammit!" The man circled to Bob's left as Bob slowly moved away from him, the tip of the knife only a foot from Bob's face.

Archie's right front paw inadvertently dislodged the door handle while the force of his large frame blew open the door. He leaped to the ground and charged toward the man, foam dripping from his muzzle. Bob caught him by the collar as the startled man retreated momentarily. Archie bared his teeth menacingly and the hair on his back stood straight up. Bob held him with both hands, straining against the dog's momentum.

The man retreated another step, tightening his grip on the knife. "Tell your damn dog to stop growling or there could be trouble for him too. Don't think I don't know how to use this thing. I'll gut him good." He pointed the knife in Archie's direction.

"Archie's just trying to protect me. You don't want to tangle with him. He's been in tougher spots than this."

"Yeah, we'll see about that. On account of I'm pretty damn good with this thing and people just tend to give me what I want." He cut the air like a swashbuckler with a sword.

Amid these wild gesticulations, Archie strained against Bob's arms and heightened his growling. Suddenly, he broke free of Bob's grasp, lunging at the man, wrapping his jaws around the knife-wielding forearm, forcing the weapon to fall. The man fell hard to the ground and screamed in agony. Archie held the arm in a vise-like grip as he straddled him.

Bob quickly picked up the knife and threw it into the nearby woods. "Archie, stop!" He yelled. Archie continued to grasp the arm, ignoring Bob. "Archie, off!" He yelled again as the man's screams grew louder. Archie continued to stand over the man, growling as he bit into the arm. "Wolfdog, no!" Bob finally exhorted him as he pulled Archie off the man. "I warned you not to mess with Archie, mister. He's part wolf. If I didn't do anything, he'd treat you like a groundhog."

As the man writhed in pain, he moaned, "Who the hell has a goddamn wolf as a pet?"

Bob shook his head. "You're lucky he didn't eat you. I suggest you get in your car and get out of here. You're better off with the police than with him."

Bob and Archie left the man where he lay as they climbed into Big Bertha and headed toward Ashtabula. Archie sat erect next to Bob, almost on his lap. Bob put his arm around Archie's back and down to his chest. The dog's heart was racing.

In a slow, measured tone, Bob said, "Great wolfdog, thank you for helping me. You protect everyone in our family. I know you will always look after us." Archie turned to Bob then licked his master's face as Bob continued to caress him.

The next morning, following Archie's first stay in a motel, they found their way to St. Joseph Cemetery where Joyce and Ed Gibson waited at their son Jimmy's grave. Bob shook their hands and introduced them to Archie who sat on command and offered a paw. "He looks like a nice dog, Bob. Just before Jimmy's accident, Joyce and I we were talking about getting him a dog. He'd done the homework. Had it narrowed down to either a shepherd or a black lab. I think Jimmy woulda liked Archie."

Bob petted Archie's head then moved to Big Bertha. He maneuvered the winch from the side of the truck and steered the heavy gravestone onto the ground above Jimmy's grave. He removed the canvas. Jimmy's parents stared at the stone without speaking. Two minutes passed in silence. Then Joyce began to cry as Ed enveloped her in his arms.

"It's Jimmy," she said through tears. "It's what he loved. He would be so happy to see this." Joyce lay some flowers near the base of the stone that displayed two crossed baseball bats above a guitar, all enclosed within a giant heart. The three of them faced the gravestone, saying nothing. Finally, Bob reached into his overall's pocket and withdrew a small stone. He placed it on top of the gravestone.

"What's that?" Joyce asked.

"Just a little custom I have. Every time I lay a monument, I bring with me a small stone from Cazenovia Lake, where I live. Originally, it was called Owagena Lake, after the Indian tribe that settled there hundreds of years ago. They had a tradition of leaving a small stone whenever they buried a member of their tribe. This meant those leaving the stone would forever be part of the dead person's journey through the afterlife. I want to remain part of Jimmy's journey."

Ed and Joyce nodded. They each picked up a pebble from the ground and placed it next to Bob's stone. They hugged Bob and petted Archie. The gravestone maker and his wolfdog climbed into

Big Bertha and headed out of the cemetery. Outside of Ashtabula as they headed on to the highway, Archie rested his head on Bob's lap.

"Great wolfdog, I've been doing some thinking. Things at home are not like I thought they'd turn out. I love our kids but my heart does not jump when I see their mother. We have been drifting in different directions for some time. I don't know the solution. Maybe I need to be on my own for a while to see if I can figure things out. While I'm gone I will need you to watch over everyone. It won't be easy with Betty. She doesn't see you like I do. I can only hope she comes around."

Archie looked at Bob then returned his head to Bob's lap as he fell asleep. A light snow began to fall. Bob would recount to his family the laying of Jimmy Gibson's marker but he never mentioned how Archie saved his life.

12.   Lifesaver

Dooley had arrayed their gear across the floor. Boy Scout Troop 18 would leave in the morning for a three day camping trip. Archie moved from one pile to the next sniffing everything.

Betty appeared from the kitchen, wearing the checkered apron. "How's it going boys? Do you have everything? Don't forget extra socks and long underwear. It's going to be pretty cold this weekend."

"Yeah, we're okay, Mom," Dooley replied. "Mr. Evans told us what to pack. And guess what? He said the footbridges at Chittenango Falls need a lot of work and that if we do a good job we can earn pioneering merit badge. You need that for Eagle, you know."

"I had no idea." Betty raised her eyebrows and gave a thumbs up as she nodded in approval. "Sounds like you have a good plan. Well, Art Evans knows scouting more than anyone around here. A shame he doesn't have any kids of his own. Pay attention. You'll learn a lot from him, boys."

Dooley stood up amid their gear. He smiled at Bob, then posed as if holding a pipe in his mouth. He put one hand on his hip and began to walk back and forth across the den. Lowering his voice, he pointed an index finger in the air. "Men, you have an important mission on this excursion. We head to Chittenango Falls. They have foot bridges over the creek we need to repair. This can be a dangerous place so we need to be aware of our surroundings at all times. Some of you will earn an important merit badge if you follow orders and do a good job. Understood? What is the scout motto?"

Betty laughed. "That's a pretty good imitation of Art, Dooley. Maybe you should go into acting." Bob held his hand to his mouth, chuckling.

"Well, finish up here. Dinner will be ready in half an hour. Then, you have your regular scout meeting at seven, right?" The boys nodded.

After cleaning the dishes fast, Bob, Dooley and Archie made a beeline for the Troop 18 lodge.

Art Evans was a long, angular man in his sixties with a gray crewcut and sideburns that reached halfway down his jaw. "Men, we leave tomorrow morning and return noon Sunday. Is everybody packed? Who's been to Chittenango Falls before?" Half the scouts raised their hands.

"We're going to hike pretty close to the falls and they run fast year round. From the center of the park it's only about a half mile before the creek drops 167 feet over glacial bedrock. I wouldn't want to take that ride." Eyes widened and heads turned as the scouts rubbed their hands together in anticipation. Dooley raised his eyebrows and Bob nodded.

The boys returned home around nine. Archie stood watching the conversation between Betty and the boys, raising his head, turning it from side to side whenever his name came up. He moved next to Bob, nuzzling his nose against Bob's thigh. "See? He knows we're talking about him. Archie knows he's coming. He's the troop's mascot!" Betty stood, arms crossed.

The next morning, Bob and Dooley zipped their jackets, adjusted their backpacks so they were comfortable and put on the matching hats and mittens Betty had knitted. Betty hugged the boys then placed her hands on Bob's shoulders. "Bob, keep an eye on your brother, understand?"

"Mom, don't worry. We're scouts. We'll be fine. And we got Archie with us. Right, boy?" Archie circled the boys excitedly, his tail wagging nonstop.

Betty looked at Archie, raised her eyebrows and pursed her lips. "Okay, see you Sunday. Be safe."

The sun shined brightly and their boots crunched on the snow as they made their way through downtown and along River Road to the scout lodge about a mile away.

"What's the scout motto, men?" Art asked, looking about the room at his young charges.

"Be prepared!" they shouted in unison, at which point Archie rose and walked around the circle of boys, nuzzling several of them. All of them gave Archie a vigorous pat on the head.

"Okay," Art continued, "let's make sure we have everything we need. You'll take turns carrying a tent. They're heavy so take care when you hike with one. They'll make your backpack top heavy."

They loaded their backpacks into a small school bus the city had donated to the troop. The boys milled around as Archie inspected everything, wagging his tail and sniffing the backpacks no doubt for some delicacy he might enjoy, approaching each boy as they rubbed his head. Archie leaped into the bus last, jumping over Bob to sit near the window. Art fired up the engine and they pulled away from the lodge.

Along the route, the boys tussled with each other and told jokes. Bob pulled off Parnell Hughes' hat and gave him a noogie. Archie looked out the window, his ears straightening from time to time whenever any wild animal appeared in a field.

Art maintained a steady pace right at the speed limit of forty. "Any of you boys know Chittenango's most famous citizen?"

The boys stopped their horseplay and looked up front at Art.

"Have you all seen the Wizard of Oz?" Art looked in the rearview mirror to see the boys nod in unison. "Well, Frank Baum, who wrote it, was from right here in Chittenango. Didn't know you were going to such a famous place, did you?"

Just then, Pete Mapes stood in the back of the bus and launched into a full-throated version of, "If I were king of the forest....."

The boys responded, "Not prince, not, duke, not earl."

Pete asked, "What would you do with a hippopotamus?"

A chorus of voices replied, "I'd tear him from top to bottomus."

"What would you do with a brontosaurus?" Pete continued.

"I'd show him who was king of the forest!" came the reply in unison.

The boys tumbled on each other laughing. Archie barked at the commotion looking at Bob, then Dooley to assure himself this was all in good fun. Forty-five minutes later, they reached their destination.

Art assembled them at the trailhead. "Men, you've camped when it was warm but winter is a different story. The conditions can be hard on your hands and feet. A scout has to be prepared for all seasons. Everybody wearing two pair of socks? And check your boot laces." The boys looked at each other then back at Art, nodding in unison. "Good. We'll hike about an hour into the woods before we set up camp. Follow the blue blazes on trees. Stay together. Bob, you and Archie bring up the rear."

As they hiked in a single file through six-inch deep snow, Archie roamed about, his nose to the ground, his ears perked at attention. He darted into the underbrush at small movements, never reappearing with any victims in his mouth. He ran to the front to see Art then circled back to Dooley and Bob. One of the boys claimed he saw a fox. Several saw deer. Archie never strayed far from the boys.

Two hours later they reached a clearing thirty yards from Chittenango Creek. "Men, set up camp here," Art declared. "Clear a place for your tents and get'em up. Once you've done that, gather some firewood. We're gonna fix the closest bridge while we still have daylight."

The scouts took fallen boughs of pine trees and swept areas in a broom-like motion to clear spots for their tents before setting them up. They used their hatchets and small saws to cut and stack firewood in neat piles of kindling, smaller branches and big logs. They started a small fire to cook soup. The temperature hovered near thirty. Archie roamed the camp perimeter, his nose close to the ground. While the boys had a snack of soup and crackers, Archie enjoyed one of the ham bones Bob had brought. The scouts then inspected the first rickety foot bridge over Chittenango Creek. It had not been tended in years and many of the fourteen-foot long thin tree trunks had grown rotten and begun to splinter. The rope that held the three-foot wide bridge together likewise had frayed. There were no hand railings.

The creek moved swiftly beneath the footbridge. A half mile away, the scouts heard the constant roar of Chittenango Falls cascading over large rock formations.

The scouts scoured the area for fallen trees and used their hatchets to trim off the branches. Art used a small saw to get an even cut at the base of trees they would use to replace the old timbers on the bridge. Once in place after removing the old timbers, he stood on each trunk, jumping up and down to ensure it did not bend and would be suitably strong. They needed six thick limbs to replace the rotten ones. Two scouts carried each trunk. Art crossed to the other side with Bob and they removed the old rope as they pulled off the old logs and threw them aside. They looped new rope around the replaced logs, up and around each one, to ensure they would stay in place. By a half hour before sunset, the scouts had finished the new bridge. Finally, each boy crossed the bridge and smiled at their collective craftsmanship before returning back to their campsite.

"Well done, men," Art said as he clapped his hands together then lit his corncob pipe. "That bridge should last until some of *your* boys are scouts." The boys smiled at one another, some of them removing their mittens to shake hands. That night, under a starry sky, they sat around the campfire eating s'mores and telling stories. At bedtime Archie settled in with Dooley, Bob and Parnell Hughes in their tent. Occasionally he darted out the front flap to roam outside whenever he heard noise, returning to sleep at the boys' feet.

After a hearty breakfast of sausage and pancakes, Art gathered the scouts in a circle once they threw snow on the fire and loaded up their backpacks. "Men, we're gonna cross that bridge you just made and hike an hour or so to our next stop to work on those hand railings near the falls. If you didn't carry a tent yesterday, today is your turn." Dooley tied the heavy canvas tent atop his backpack.

At the footbridge, Art led the way as the scouts crossed single file. Archie and Bob brought up the rear. Dooley approached the bridge just in front of Bob then paused. "Go ahead, Bob, I gotta tie this boot, I'll be right there."

Bob looked down at Dooley's boot. "Okay, I'll wait for you on the other side; Mr. Evans wants Archie and me at the back."

Dooley bent over to tie his lace and almost tipped over. He knelt and tied his lace in a double knot. He grabbed onto a nearby sapling to pull himself up, adjusted the backpack, pulled up his mittens and stared ahead at the three by fourteen foot passageway. No handrails to steady himself and below the sound of the fast moving creek. In the distance, the constant roar of the falls permeated the still forest.

Dooley approached the bridge gingerly, taking small steps, his arms extended like the wings of an airplane. He mumbled to himself, "No big deal, only fourteen feet, I can do it. Just look at the other side and I'll be with the others." He tried not to look at the swiftly flowing water with the steep banks on both sides. But the creek mesmerized him, its constant motion and drone drew him to the center like a hypnotist's spinning wheel. The snow on the logs was packed from the footsteps of the other scouts and proved slippery. Dooley looked up to the other side and saw Bob and Archie about thirty yards ahead.

Bob had stopped in the path made by the others and was throwing a stick that Archie chased. He looked back at Dooley tiptoeing across the bridge before turning to move ahead a little more. Art and the other scouts were another thirty yards ahead of Bob.

Dooley stayed to the middle of the footbridge. He paused momentarily to adjust his backpack. He skidded but caught himself. Sweat raised on his temples. His heart raced suddenly. He paused, then tried walking sideways, shuffling his feet like at basketball practice being careful not to cross them. Halfway across. Just another seven feet.

Suddenly, his left foot stubbed a small bit of branch protruding from a log. He started to lean toward the creek. He felt the tent shift to his left shoulder throwing him off balance. He tried to stand but the backpack and tent slid toward his head. His right foot slipped on the wet logs and all of a sudden he plunged over the side and fell four feet into the frigid water.

Completely submerged in the six-foot deep current, the weight of the soaked backpack dragged him to the silty bottom. He tried to shed it but his arms could not grab the straps tied at his waist in a square knot that held the heavy load in place. Everything was black. He felt the soft bottom and pushed off, getting his head to rise just above the surface. He gasped for air and tried to scream for help but the words barely left his chattering lips. He kicked his legs as fast as he could to keep his head above the swift current that carried him downstream. The roar of the falls grew louder. He spit our freezing water as fast as it flowed in his mouth. Dooley stayed toward the middle of the creek. He flailed his arms trying to keep his head above water.

Archie sniffed the ground near Bob. Suddenly his ears shot straight upward, he lifted his head high and turned toward the creek giving a guttural bark before bolting in that direction. Bob looked back toward the footbridge. Dooley was nowhere in sight. As he jerked off his backpack, he shouted, "Mr. Evans, I don't see Dooley. " Then Bob took off after Archie, a black and tan blur of fur running thirty yards in front of him.

Dooley struggled to stay afloat, managing a plaintive 'help' every other breath. Chittenango Falls lie 120 yards ahead and their rumble heightened. Dooley's arms were weakening by the second and even if he had the strength, there were no overhanging branches to grab onto to halt his steady journey toward the cascades.

Archie bolted through the underbrush, the hair on his back raised. As if shot from a cannon, ears pinned back, muscles tensed, he sped toward the creek. Leaping through the dense forest alongside the creek, he dodged trees in his path covering five feet at a leap.

Fifty feet away from Archie, Dooley continued to kick his legs, now more slowly, but his arms would not move. He arched his back so his mouth could take in air. The falls grew louder, now less than one hundred yards away.

Archie made for an opening in the trees. He jumped midstride onto a large fallen pine alongside the creek bank. Flexing his powerful hind legs he used the tree as a springboard and exploded ten feet through the air into the water, front and back legs fully extended. Once he landed, his legs moved like an engine's pistons. He swam with the current, reaching Dooley then bit into the backpack.

Dooley felt himself being steered toward the creek bank. A large branch extended low over the water. Dooley strained to grab it but his arms would not cooperate. They felt like fifty pound weights were attached to them. Finally, Archie gained a foothold in the soft silt along the bank and the two of them halted. Dooley struggled to raise his arms and grabbed an overhanging branch.

Archie's jaws remained firmly implanted in the tent. Dooley closed his eyes nearing exhaustion. His teeth chattered nonstop. Turning his head he saw Archie. He tried putting one arm around Archie's neck but failed. Archie would not budge. His strength prevented the two of them from rejoining the current.

Moments later, Bob arrived first on the scene. He extended his body onto the low branch and grabbed his brother's arm. "You're okay Dooley. I'm gonna get you out. Let go of the branch. Archie, let go, boy. I got him."

Dooley released his weak grip as Archie let go of the tent. Archie climbed out of the water and shook his body. Bob used all his strength to pull Dooley to a sitting position and his feet remained in the water. Just then Art and a few scouts arrived and helped Bob lift Dooley completely out of the water and remove his backpack.

No one spoke for a few seconds. Dooley crawled the few feet to Archie and enveloped the dog in his arms as he buried his head into Archie's wet chest. "Archie," he whispered, the words escaping through chattering teeth. Archie licked the tears on Dooley's face.

Art began to rub Dooley's legs. "Bob, you and Eddie rub Dooley's arms. We have to get him warm. Parnell, go back with four others, get your gear, then cross back over the footbridge and start a fire where we camped last night. Paul, set up a tent. We need to get Dooley out of these clothes and warm him up by a fire. Joe, you and Lucas get two blankets from our packs and bring them here, right away. Double time, everyone! Let's go!"

Within a few minutes, Joe and Lucas returned with the blankets. Art wrapped Dooley in one while Bob covered Archie with the other. Archie would not leave Dooley's side. Art removed his hat and rubbed his temples. "Dooley, can you feel your fingers and toes okay?" Dooley nodded through chattering teeth. Turning to Archie he stroked the dog's head. "You earned lifesaving merit badge today, Archie."

After twenty minutes, Dooley regained enough circulation to walk back the half mile to the previous night's campsite. He held

Bob's arm crossing the bridge, looking down into the water. "Bob, what if Archie didn't jump in to get me? What would have happened?"

"Don't think about it. Just be glad Archie *was* there."

Shortly thereafter, the scouts created a roaring fire and set up a tent. Inside it, they removed Dooley's wet clothes and boots, and gave him someone's dry sweatshirt and long underwear. Art prepared some hot chicken soup for Dooley then carefully felt the boy's extremities. "Can you feel everything okay, son?" Dooley closed his eyes and sighed as he nodded.

The scouts fashioned some branches near the fire to dry as much as possible Dooley's backpack and gear. Bob gave Archie a ham bone, keeping him happily occupied.

Art surveyed the scene. "Men, we'll hike back to the bus once Dooley feels up to walking. He doesn't have extra boots so we can't have him hiking very long in wet ones. We'll come back in the warmer weather to finish those jobs. We'll divide up his gear to carry. Let's just get him home."

They made their way back to the bus. Archie walked alongside Dooley every step of the way and sat next to him on the ride back to Cazenovia. The journey proceeded quietly in contrast to the raucous trip there singing 'Wizard of Oz' songs. Art dropped off each scout at his house then drove Bob, Dooley and Archie home.

The boys tumbled into the house with Archie and Art trailing. Betty put down the Christmas stocking she was knitting and approached the doorway as it jarred open. Her eyes widened and her back straightened. The Irish twins squealed with delight as Archie approached them and licked their faces. Patrick walked down the stairs in his Hopalong Cassidy outfit.

"Boys, you're home early. I thought you were camping until Sunday." She furrowed her brow and clasped her hands together. "Art, thank you for bringing them. Is everything okay?"

"Well, Betty, we had a little accident."

Bob blurted out, "Mom, Archie saved Dooley! It was unbelievable. Dooley was gonna go over Chittenango Falls!"

"Dear God!" Betty exclaimed, her hands covering her chin before she lowered them and gripped Dooley by the shoulders turning him in a full circle. Dooley dumped his wet backpack with a thud on the floor. Betty moved her hands up and down her son.

Dooley, embarrassed by this attention, stepped back from his mother. "Mom, I'm okay. I just had a little accident. But if it wasn't for Archie, I wouldn't be okay. I could've gone over the waterfalls. I was pretty scared."

Betty turned to Art with a knit brow and pursed lips. "Art, what happened here? How could you let that happen?"

Art bowed his head, staring at his feet, his face reddened, and he ran his right hand through his gray crewcut. Shifting his weight from one foot to the other, "Well, Betty, we had a little mishap. Dooley fell into the creek, uh, tripped crossing a footbridge. Thankfully, Archie came to the rescue. He, uh, pulled Dooley off to the side until we arrived. Wouldn't let go of Dooley until Bob told him it was okay."

Betty looked again at Dooley and closed her eyes and whispered, "Mary, Mother of God."

Art avoided Betty's eyes. "Betty, I'm uh real sorry this happened. First time in my thirty years of scouting. Thankfully, we had a guardian angel with us. And that was Archie. Thank God, Dooley's gonna be fine. " He shifted his eyes up to her face, finally able to return her stone-faced gaze. "Yeah, Dooley's gonna be okay." Betty stood staring at him, as still as a rock. She let Art out with a sharp look and no further words.

Betty closed the door and sank back into the rocking chair, the full realization of what might have happened finally hitting her. She took a deep breath. The Irish twins swarmed around her as Patrick hugged Archie. Almost in unison they stared at Bob and Dooley and clamored, "Tell us what happened! Everything. How big were the waterfalls? How did Archie know what to do? Start at the beginning and don't leave anything out."

"Mom," Bob said excitedly, "It was like being in a real life adventure of Rin-Tin-Tin. We were crossing the footbridge we fixed and all of a sudden I didn't see Dooley on account of he tripped and fell in the river." Patrick's eyes grew as big as silver dollars. "Yeah, and then I saw Archie racing toward the waterfalls. Boy, were they loud. I couldn't see Dooley and I think I might have heard him cry help, but I'm not sure. Dooley, did you cry help?"

"Yeah, but my teeth were chattering and I had all this water going in my mouth. So you probably couldn't hear it." Betty's eyes widened and she clasped her hand across her mouth, suppressing a cry.

Bob continued. "Anyways, I'm running behind Archie and all of a sudden I see him leap through the air, like Superman, and then he disappears. I can't see him. But I hear a big splash, even louder than the sound of the falls. So I'm really worried now 'cause I know Archie's in the river and so is Dooley. So, I kept running toward them. The next thing I see when I get to the river is Archie and Dooley. Archie's biting Dooley's backpack and has his body against Dooley's so they can't go downstream more. I pulled Dooley out and then we wrapped Dooley and Archie in blankets. And then Mr. Evans made Dooley chicken soup and we gave him dry clothes to put on. Everybody was saying Archie was a real hero. Just like you see on TV."

Dooley looked over at Archie playing with the girls. "All I know is, I'm sure glad Archie was with us." Archie rose at the sound of his name and approached Dooley, nuzzling him before returning to the Irish twins. "I don't like to think what would have happened if he didn't save me."

Betty let out a strangled little cry and her eyes welled up. Then she shook her head and composed herself before opening her arms to engulf Bob and Dooley. "Yes, it was quite an adventure but thank goodness it's over, and you are all right. Well, you boys should hang up that wet gear in the back room. Then, we'll have something warm to eat."

Dooley and Bob gathered their gear and headed to the storage room near the garage to hang things to dry. Patrick and the Irish twins followed them. Patrick's spurs on his cowboy boots jangled as he spit out a slew of questions. "Bob, how did Archie know Dooley was in trouble? Wasn't Archie afraid of the river and getting cold? How far from the waterfalls were they when Archie stopped Dooley?"

"Patrick," Bob looked over his shoulder at his younger brother, "You help us hang this stuff and we'll tell you everything."

Betty stood as she watched her children wind their way to the back of the house. Her face was pale and her body began to shake uncontrollably. She eased herself into the chair, shuddered, put her hands across her face, leaned her head against the high back and closed her eyes. After a moment she opened them, picked up her knitting needles and the Christmas stocking and saw Archie reclining next to the sofa. Archie lifted his head as he looked at her. His tail thumped once, then he lowered his head back onto his paws, looking away. He probably had no reason to expect Betty to come near him. She put down the knitting and stood up.

Dooley, meanwhile, told Bob, "My feet are kind of cold. I'm going up to our room and get some warmer socks. I'll come back in a second to help you." He went up the back stairs, got some socks and started to return to the back room by the front steps when he stopped near the top as he watched his mother do something he had never seen.

Betty approached Archie and knelt at his side. She stroked his large head and looked into his brown eyes. Archie closed his eyes, then applied pressure against Betty's hand. She put her arms around his neck and buried her head into his fur. Tears streamed down her cheeks. "Archie, thank you." Archie turned to face Betty once she loosened her grip, her face just inches from his. He licked the salty tears from her cheeks then nestled his head in her lap.

13.   Sudden Changes

Big Bob arrived home from the shop near five that afternoon. He removed his dust -covered boots and hung up his heavy canvas work jacket on the hooks above the floor register. He stretched his arms skyward to loosen the kinks in his shoulders after a day of sand-blasting. He glanced around the partition into the living room and raised his eyebrows on seeing Archie stretched out on the floor at Betty's feet. Betty rocked gently while knitting a red, white and green two-foot long Christmas stocking and humming a song. Bob raised his head to sniff what he suspected was roast beef cooking in the oven. His stomach made an audible sound as he hung his jacket near the door. He had subsisted all day on black coffee and Salems fortified with a few chasers of Canadian Club whiskey.

Archie lifted his head, rose slowly, stretched the length of his body, yawned and approached Bob. The large man knelt down to eye level with Archie then massaged the dog's neck and ears. Archie moved his head in a circle.

"Where are the kids, Betty?"

Without looking up at him she replied, "The girls are upstairs with Timmer. Patrick asked to go with Bob and Dooley to deliver Archie's papers. They left Archie here so he wouldn't get confused over not delivering papers. Patrick wants to learn the route for when the boys go on camping trips."

"I thought the boys were supposed to be at Chittenango Falls camping until tomorrow."

Continuing to focus on her knitting, she pointed to a chair. "Sit down, Bob, I want to tell you something."

"Okay. C'mon, Archie, let's let you out so you're not in your mother's hair."

"No. Archie can stay," Betty said matter of factly as she put her knitting in the bag beside her chair and finally looked her husband who approached a seat on the opposite side of the room. "He's the reason I want to talk with you."

Bob stiffened, gripping the arms of the chair his knuckles turned white as he lowered his six foot four frame into it. Then, momentarily rising, his face reddened. "Oh, Betty, come on. I've had a long day. I don't need another one of your lectures about Archie....or me, for that matter." He glared at his wife who looked back at him with the enigma of a sphinx.

Betty folded her hands on her lap then pointed to his chair. "Sit down, Bob. Archie's not going anywhere...... ever." She paused a moment and added, "We'll talk about you later."

Bob sank back in his chair, speechless. He rubbed his temples then raised his voice. "What's going on here? What do you mean, ever? But....but you despise Archie!"

"Not any more. Archie will be an important member of this family until he dies. And no one will love him more than I." She held Bob's gaze.

Bob blended into the threadbare stuffed chair. He rubbed his eyes with the heels of his hands, then blurted out, "Betty, I'm not ready for some stupid psychological game. You've hated Archie since Dooley and I brought him through that door four years ago!" Bob pointed to the front door. "The boys and I do everything we can to keep him out of your way. I don't know what your game is here but we've done our part." Bob's eyes narrowed and his lips tightened. He shook his head and held his calloused hands skyward as if appealing to some higher being. "And all of a sudden you love him?" Archie lay on the floor between them constantly moving his head back and forth following the voice.

"Archie saved Dooley's life."

Again, his jaw dropped. Mouth open, he stared down at Archie who had been giving Bob undivided attention during his outbursts. Bob turned back to Betty whose blue-green eyes were laser beams penetrating his body. "What are you talking about, Betty?"

"Dooley fell off a footbridge into Chittenango Creek and was headed toward the falls. Archie jumped in after him and pulled him to the side until Art and the other boys caught up. Art said only an act of God prevented Dooley from going over those falls. God.....and Archie."

Beads of sweat formed on Bob's hairline. His fingers tingled. Bob took a deep breath then reached down and stroked the head and back of the huge dog. "I knew he was special from the moment I saw him, Betty. I just had no idea how special. I never told you this but back when Archie and I went to Ohio to set Jimmy's stone, we pulled over to help a guy who seemed in distress. I left Archie in the truck while I saw what was going on. The guy pulled a knife on me demanding money. Archie somehow hit the door handle and got out and jumped on the guy before he could use the knife. Now, both Dooley and I owe Archie our lives."

He looked at Betty. They both nodded.

That night for dinner Betty had prepared a pot roast with oven browned potatoes, mixed carrots and green beans accompanied by homemade biscuits and apple crisp for dessert. "Betty, that was one of your finest dinners," Big Bob said as he loosened his belt buckle a notch then sat back in his chair and nursed a black coffee. Patrick rubbed his belly and nodded.

"Sure was a lot better than what we had camping the other night," Dooley added.

As Bob and Dooley cleared the plates and moved to the trash can to toss the scraps, Betty blurted out, "Boys, don't throw that. I'm sure Archie would like it. Just put it in his bowl."

The boys looked at each other and raised their eyebrows. "Are you sure, Mom?" Dooley asked.

She nodded.

The boys shrugged their shoulders and moved in unison to Archie's bowl where they dumped the leftovers. Archie rose and paused cautiously at his bowl. He had received his dinner an hour earlier.

Patrick had been sitting quietly, observing everything. He looked up at Betty. "Mommy, do you like Archie now?"

Suddenly, you could hear a pin drop. All eyes turned toward Betty. She might as well have been thrust on to a dark stage with a bright spotlight blinding her from the audience.

Betty straightened her back in the chair, took the napkin from her lap and dabbed the corners of her mouth. Slowly, she folded her hands, paused for five seconds then turned to Patrick. "Well, Patrick, I've thought about Archie a lot today. You know he did something very special for this family that very few dogs could ever do. He saved your brother. Who knows what would have happened to Dooley if he had fallen over the water falls. But he didn't because Archie was his guardian angel."

Patrick interrupted. "Yeah, but Mom, can dogs really be angels? Sister Mary Catherine never said anything about dogs being angels. Not even once. She prob'ly knows a lot about that angel stuff."

"I'm sure she does, sweetheart. But you can tell her your mother thinks Archie is a guardian angel for this family. He will always be loved and he will always be with us."

Dooley approached Betty and placed his hand on her right shoulder. "Mom, are you saying if Archie does something wrong he won't have to go live on that farm?"

"That will never happen, Dooley. Archie will always be with us. Always." Betty rose from her seat, approached Archie who had just finished his "dessert," then placed her arms around his neck and kissed the top of his head. The children's' jaws dropped and Big Bob remained speechless. Betty stood up and clapped her hands and smiled. "Okay, let's get this kitchen cleaned up. Everybody done with their homework?" Several heads nodded. "Good, when you're done here you can watch one show then upstairs to get ready for bed and read your chapter books."

The children surrounded Archie and petted him. Dooley framed Archie's head in his hands and gazed into the dog's eyes.

"Archie, you're not on pro-bra-tion anymore. You're gonna be here forever!" A group hug with Archie in the center ensued as the kids excitedly jumped up and down.

"Okay, kids," Betty said smiling, "let's get to work here."

Like miniature soldiers following orders, Dooley stacked the dishes, consolidated the silverware and grabbed a dishcloth to clean the table. Young Bob pulled out the dishwasher from the side of the sink, connected the hose to the faucet and began loading it. Patrick grabbed the broom and dustpan and swept the kitchen floor.

Betty took Timmer upstairs for his bath. Big Bob took Maureen and Lisa into the den and flicked on the TV. While he watched the Evening News with Huntley and Brinkley, the girls rolled on the floor with Archie, wrestling with him and laughing nonstop. Twenty minutes later the boys joined them to watch an episode of "Gunsmoke" before Betty turned off the TV and followed the kids up the stairs to get the younger ones ready for bed.

With the kids tucked in, Bob and Betty sat silently in the den. She returned to the Christmas stocking that was halfway done. Bob leafed through the Syracuse Herald. The tick of the second hand on the ancient grandfather clock and the crinkling of the newspaper in Bob's hands were the only sounds that pierced the silence. It had gone on like this most nights now for several months.

Betty put down her knitting, folded her hands on her lap, took a deep breath and looked at her husband. "Bob, I can't live like this anymore. Something has to change."

Bob closed his eyes and rubbed his temples. The room was dimly lit from a small table lamp. The silence was deafening. Finally, he looked up. "Betty, what do you want from me? I'm doing my best to keep things moving forward."

"Bob, we don't talk much anymore. Maybe it would do us both good if you moved in with your mother for a while."

Bob squinted at Betty. He raised his eyebrows. "Is that what you really want? Okay, we've had our problems. All couples do. That's just life."

"No, Bob, it's not just life. Other couples face their problems head on. We don't talk about ours and when we do, you seem in a haze. It's better for us and the kids if you move out. Maybe you'll change. But nothing's going to change until you stop drinking."

Bob uncrossed his legs and folded his hands. He stared at the floor. "I'm under a lot of pressure, Betty. So, I take a few drinks to take off the edge. A lot of guys do."

"Bob, you do more than take off the edge. I think you put yourself on the edge...the edge of reality. Look around you. We barely survive. I've taken a part-time job at the college to help pay the bills. I need you to give me an envelope every week with enough cash to pay the mortgage and buy some groceries."

"What are we going to tell the kids?" Bob's shoulders slumped and with his elbows leaned on his knees took both hands and rubbed his temples.

"We can tell them grandma is getting old and needs your help. They'll understand. You can come home for Sunday dinners. We'll try this for a few months and see if anything improves. Right now, I just don't want you around here." She rose and went to bed. Bob did not turn his head to follow her as she left the room. He stared at the floor.

Archie rose from his blanket and approached his master. Big Bob opened his arms and welcomed him.

"Great wolfdog, as I have told you many times, we are coming to a point where you will take on greater responsibility. I must go away for how long, I do not know. You are now fully welcome in this house. Everyone here depends upon you. I am counting on you to protect this family. I know you understand this. I must leave and you must take my place."

Archie sat and stared at Big Bob as though they were having a profound conversation. Whether he understood what the man said, we don't know. Big Bob truly believed Archie fully comprehended everything that was said. The wolfdog licked his master's hand then slowly turned and headed up the stairs to the room where Betty lay awake staring at the ceiling. He approached her bed. She reached out and stroked his head. He lay beside her on the floor and soon fell asleep.

14.   A Visitor from the City

Betty O'Neill had a soft spot for somebody facing hard times. She always reminded her children to 'be generous in small ways'. While she stretched every dollar as far as she could, it never crossed her mind that she was not in a position to help someone else. When a family in a nearby town lost their house to fire, Betty unloaded half her kids' dressers to their great surprise when they arrived from school one day. "You kids have enough to wear. You should be happy knowing other children your age who lost everything will appreciate having some clothes new to them." When Max the Milkman had a stroke, she made dinner for his family for a week.

"I have a surprise for you," she said while plopping mashed potatoes on six plates followed by a portion of overcooked meat loaf and canned green beans. "Next month we will have a young boy, Andrew Priyou, coming to stay with us for two weeks."

"How come he's staying with us, Mom?" Patrick inquired while shoveling a massive mouthful of potatoes onto his fork.

"Well, the Altar and Rosary Society at church decided to invite children from a big city to spend some time in the countryside. Andrew lives in a part of New York City called Harlem where they don't have a nice lake and lots of green space. He's coming with a group of kids to live with families. They call it the 'fresh air' project because these kids will get a real countryside experience here in Cazenovia."

"Is dad bringing him, Mom?" asked Bob.

"No, Andrew is coming on a bus. Your father needs to stay with Grandma, like we discussed a while ago. And besides, he had to go out of state to lay a marker so he won't meet Andrew."

"Where's this kid gonna sleep?" added Dooley as a green and white amalgam escaped from the corner of his mouth.

"Dooley, I told you, don't speak with food in your mouth. Swallow then speak. As a matter of fact, since he's about your age I thought he could sleep with you and Patrick."

"Do you have a picture of him? If he's going to sleep with me I'd like to know what he looks like."

"No, I don't have a picture of him. All I can tell you is that he is a Negro like all the kids coming here."

Curious looks and furrowed brows surrounded the table. Archie accepted Patrick's green beans when Betty turned to feed Timmer. Lisa spoke up. "Mommy, what's a Negro?"

"Well, honey, they're people like you and me only they have a different skin color. They're black."

"Is it 'cause they got sunburned?" Lisa continued.

"No, dear, they're born with that color."

"Then how come I never saw one?"

"I saw Negroes when we went to Shopping Town. Not a lot, but some," an authoritative Dooley contributed, nodding. Bob signaled his agreement.

Betty paused for a moment, scanning the faces around the table, all of whom waited for her to say something. "Well, it's this way, kids. No Negroes live in Cazenovia, at least not right now. But most of the people from Harlem are black. They don't have much money to visit places so this is a special vacation for Andrew." Betty turned to Patrick. "Good job with those green beans, Patrick."

He smiled like a Cheshire cat. "Do you think Andrew will like Archie, Mom?"

"Oh, I'm sure he will. I don't know if Andrew has a dog. If he does, it's probably small since Andrew lives in an apartment." Archie, hearing his name, emerged from beneath the table, stretched and surveyed the gathering. Patrick brushed away a fragment of green bean from Archie's muzzle then petted his head, smiling over another escape from vegetables.

***

A few weeks later Betty piled the kids into the rusting 1956 Dodge Coronet station wagon and headed to the high school to meet the bus from Harlem. Archie remained home, stretched out in the porch shade.

Andrew surveyed the countryside as the bus made its way from New York City to rural central New York State. Wide-eyed youngsters, aged ten to thirteen, all black and all from Harlem, spoke to each other in hushed tones as they watched farmland pass by for the first time. "This sure don't look like home," said one to another.

At mid-morning on a sultry July day, thirty youngsters filed off the bus at Cazenovia High School, each with a small rectangular suitcase with their name printed on a piece of paper pinned to their shirts. They huddled together suspiciously eying the horde of white people surrounding them. Organizers took each child to their host family. A member of the St. James altar guild led Andrew to the O'Neills. A smiling white lady in her mid-thirties bent down to Andrew's eye level and placed a welcoming arm around him.

"Andrew, I'm Betty O'Neill. We're so happy to have you with us. This is your new family for the next two weeks, Bob, Dooley, Patrick, Maureen, Lisa and this little fellow is Timmer."

Betty's children were dressed in their summer casual clothes, cut-off jean shorts, madras shirts and sneakers worn thin in the tread after a school year of gym class. New ones would come in August when they went to Shopping Town. Andrew, on the other hand, appeared in his Sunday best. He wore a short-sleeved, checkered shirt, buttoned to the neck, ankle high blue khaki pants exposing white socks and shiny black shoes. His belt looped almost halfway around his waist to his back. Eleven years old, he weighed maybe eighty pounds, skinny as a rail. His eyes nervously surveyed the gathering.

Lisa reached out to touch his forearm. He drew it back instinctively, not saying a word, large brown eyes unblinking, his legs shaking slightly.

For a few moments Betty waited to see how her children would welcome the newcomer. They stared at Andrew as though he had arrived from outer space. Andrew's eyes darted from one face to the next.

"Do you like to play baseball?" Dooley blurted out. Andrew nodded silently.

"How about swimming?" Patrick added. "We have a good lake here." Andrew shrugged his shoulders.

Betty knelt down and put her arm around his shoulders. "You know, kids, Andrew has had a long trip from Harlem. Let's go home and get him settled, shall we?" Everyone nodded.

They silently filed into the wagon with Andrew in front between Betty and Bob. Dooley held Timmer while Patrick, Maureen and Lisa leaned forward, staring at the new kid to see if he would speak. Lisa gently put her hand on Andrew's close-cropped hair. "Your hair is soft like a new brush. It feels different than our hair." Andrew recoiled slightly and did not turn to look back.

"Andrew is the same as we are, Lisa, only a different color, that's all," Betty spoke without removing her eyes from the road.

They pulled into the driveway. Archie stopped chewing a football on the porch, jumped up excitedly and loped toward the car. They piled out, surrounding Andrew who gazed at the house, mouth agape. At the sight of a new face, Archie bounded to Andrew, jumping up on him, his paws on Andrew's shoulders. Startled, he fell back into Betty as Archie lapped the boy's chin.

"Bob, get Archie," Betty said urgently. Andrew trembled in her arms. Bob grabbed Archie's collar, pulling him away from the quivering boy.

Andrew's knees bumped together in a steady rhythm. His hazel eyes dilated. His hands shook involuntarily. He stared at the huge dog who outweighed him by fifty pounds.

Betty knelt, cradling him. "Now, Andrew, you haven't met the most important member of our family. This is Archie. When you get to know him, you and he will be best friends."

Andrew took an enormous breath, as though preparing to swim a pool length underwater, then exhaled his first words since arriving, "Ma'am, how long you 'pose it's gonna take that dog to get to know me?"

"Archie is very gentle, Andrew. You and he will get to know each other in no time at all. You'll have a wonderful time with him." Andrew's knees gradually stopped shaking and his breathing returned to normal. He watched Lisa approach Archie and hug him tightly around the neck.

"Nice puppy," Lisa purred and giggled as Archie returned the affection, licking her face, his huge tongue lubricating half her face.

Andrew raised his eyebrows and looked to Betty. "That Archie, he don't bite people?"

"Oh, no, Andrew, Archie loves people. He's never bitten anyone. Everyone in Cazenovia likes Archie. Right kids?"

Bob piped up. "Oh, yeah, Mom. That's easy. How many dogs get to go into the hardware store and drug store on their own and even deliver newspapers? How many dogs are Boy Scout mascots? How many dogs get treats from the school principal? How many dogs are part wolf?"

Dooley piped in, "Heck, how many dogs save somebody's life?" Bob nodded at Dooley who proceeded to kneel down and hug Archie.

Andrew looked at Bob and Dooley questioningly, his eyebrows knit together. "You sayin' Archie is part wolf and he actually saved somebody's life?"

Dooley looked up at Andrew. "That's me. Archie saved me from going over a waterfall."

Andrew's mouth refused to close. If his eyes could have grown bigger, they would have dropped out of his head. "He did all that and he a wolfdog too?"

"Yup," Bob said matter of factly. "Archie's a hero around here. The scout leader even gave him a medal. He might look a little scary to some people on account of him being so big. Most people don't know he's part wolf. We don't advertise that part. " Andrew continued to stare at Archie.

"Okay, kids. Andrew will have time to get to know Archie. He just needs to get used to being around such a big dog. C'mon Andrew, let's get you settled. After that, I thought we could have a picnic at the lake. Would you like that?"

Andrew composed himself as he surveyed his new 'family'. His furrowed brow moved from face to face until it settled on a panting Archie. "I ain't never seen no animal big as him in my whole life." Andrew's legs became steadier and his hands stopped shaking. He wiped a few beads of sweat from his hairline then took another deep breath and said in a low, measured tone, "I like picnics but if we're going to your lake I don't know how to swim."

"No problem," Betty said smiling, "Bob and Dooley can teach you. They learned how to swim in the scouts. They'll have you swimming in no time!"

Once they got Andrew settled in Dooley and Patrick's room, Betty packed a picnic basket. They learned Andrew had not brought a swim suit so they put him in one of Dooley's. It hung low on Andrew's hips reaching below his knees and billowed around his thighs. The string wrapped almost twice around his waist. Somehow, he managed to keep it on. They walked the three blocks to the lake. Archie trailed behind. Andrew looked back every minute to make sure the huge dog remained at a safe distance.

At the lake, Andrew told Betty he could start swim lessons another day. Archie sat near the wading area about thirty yards from where Betty laid their blanket and placed bologna and mustard sandwiches on a paper plate next to an open bag of potato chips and a thermos of Kool-Aid. Archie turned his head back and forth watching children come and go.

While Betty made small talk with Andrew and he mumbled 'uh-huh' from time to time, the young boy watched Archie interact with many children. When a mother turned her attention to a friend and her toddler crawled at an Olympian pace to the water, Archie trotted across the sand and positioned himself between the child and the water to block its progress as the mother hurried to pick up the youngster and petted Archie on the head and thanked him for helping.

Andrew noticed everyone seemed comfortable with Archie. The dog moved easily from family to family, where some mothers offered him a cracker or other treat, the children petted him, and others stroked his huge head with seemingly assuring tones. Andrew turned to Betty. "All these people, they know your Archie. Where I live, people got a lot of mean dogs. We got no Archie there." Betty smiled at him and reassuringly rubbed his back.

That night in bed, Dooley and Andrew told stories before falling asleep. Patrick listened intently from a nearby bed. "Me and my two older brothers sleep in one bed at home," Andrew told Dooley. "And my grandma, she lives with us. My momma, she works in a tall building making sure those offices are real clean. She does a good job."

Archie entered the room as they talked, nuzzled Patrick then walked over to Dooley and Andrew's single bed. Dooley sat up, hugging the dog who returned the love licking Dooley's face profusely. Archie then jumped partially on the bed, as the bedsprings squeaked under his sudden weight, his front paws crossing Dooley's body until he came face to face with Andrew. Archie sniffed the boy.

Andrew recoiled instantly trying to blend into the wall. He paused for thirty seconds while looking at the gently panting dog.

Dooley looked at Andrew. "It's okay. You don't have to worry about Archie. He'd never hurt you." Gingerly, Andrew leaned over Dooley and placed his hand on Archie's large head, caressing the soft ears. Archie angled his head backwards, seeming to enjoy the attention. "Archie likes you, Andrew," Dooley said smiling. Andrew continued petting Archie and he returned Dooley's smile.

"I don't have no dog at home and I never seen one like Archie."

"Tell you what," Dooley replied, "how about you and I go around town tomorrow and you can lead Archie."

Andrew smiled and nodded. "I'd like that. I never walked no dog before."

The next day the two boys accompanied Archie on a walkabout. "We don't have a leash," Dooley told Andrew. "On account of everybody in town knows Archie and he pretty much goes where he wants. But I think this time we'll attach this rope to Archie's collar and you can walk him. That way, he'll get to know you better." Andrew took the rope cautiously and felt the large dog strain against it. He grabbed it with both hands. Archie's head was almost level with Andrew's chest. "You know, Andrew, you can talk to Archie. He'll listen to you. He's real smart."

"Archie, I know you not used to this rope, but you got to go with me." Archie looked back at his new master then made a move to run toward downtown, almost pulling Andrew off his feet. "Stop," the boy shouted, digging in his heels to restrain the huge dog. "Now, you go slower or I gonna pull on this rope." Archie stared at Andrew, then turned to Dooley, who smiled at Archie. Andrew shortened his grip on the rope so Archie was at his side. They walked slowly. Andrew nodded to Dooley. "I think Archie likes me. He doing what I tell him."

"Archie definitely likes you. You just need more time with him. It's like having another brother, if you know what I mean. He just wants to be with us." Dooley paused to envelope Archie's head in both hands. "Archie, we're gonna give you a couple of weeks off from delivering the newspapers so you and Andrew can be together a lot." The dog looked up at Dooley and wagged his tail.

Andrew stopped in his tracks with a look of surprise crossing his face as Archie also halted and sat next to Andrew. "You sayin' Archie actually delivers newspapers?"

"Oh, yeah. He's got his own houses. We roll up the papers then put one in his mouth and he takes it to the right house every time. Makes our job go super-fast."

Andrew stared at Archie. "Dooley, I think Archie must be human inside. He do what people do. He smarter than some of the people I go to school with. And he a wolf too and he don't bite. I'm gonna tell people at home 'bout Archie. Where you get him?"

"My dad and I got him about six years ago from this guy who breeds dogs. He told us a girl shepherd escaped her pen and had a baby with a real live wolf, like a wild one, you know. Then, my dad sees this puppy and they start to talk to each other in this secret language only they understand."

Andrew furrowed his brow. "You sayin' your dad talks to dogs?"

"Well, maybe not all dogs, I don't know about that. But he and Archie, they understand each other. Archie got lost once when he was just a puppy and he told my dad about fighting wild animals to save himself. Dad told us everything. Look at Archie's ear. See the part that's chopped off at the tip? That was from a fight."

Andrew stood with his mouth wide open. "Archie, he got a lot of stories. And your dad, he must have some kind of special powers or something. I never heard of no dog talker before. How you think he does it?"

"I don't know. Late at night my dad says he and Archie spend time alone and somehow they talk to each other. I guess it must be some kind of magic. Maybe it's because Archie is part wolf."

Andrew looked at Archie, then back at Dooley. "There's lots of things I'm learning that don't happen where I come from. Your mom, she prob'ly happy to have such a smart dog."

Dooley frowned. "Well, not quite. She's okay now but we almost didn't get to keep Archie."

Andrew raised his eyebrows. "How come? Your mom, she seems real nice. She looks like she likes Archie okay. He seem like the perfect dog. How come she didn't like him?"

"Yeah, well, let's say Archie had some bad habits."

"Like what. I don't see nothin'."

"My mom works for the president of the college now. She's some kind of special helper. Well, the president learned Archie was stealing tennis balls that flew over the fence when their team practiced."

Andrew shrugged and held his palms upward. "That doesn't sound so bad. They're just balls. So he chews a few, so what?"

"We found a hundred and fifty behind the garage."

Andrew's eyebrows shot upward and his mouth opened in a wide oval. He looked down at Archie. "I can see where your mom would be angry with that."

"Well," Dooley replied, "that's nothing. Then he ate our turkey for Thanksgiving dinner when nobody was looking. Ate the whole thing. Dad took him outside and he barfed big time. Bob and I had to clean it up. Really gross." Dooley held his nose and shook his head.

Andrew put his hand over his mouth and giggled then suddenly halted in his tracks, causing Archie to stop as well. Andrew's eyes bulged and he retreated slightly from the dog. "I see Archie does some bad things. Maybe that the wolf comin' out in him. But he don't bite people?"

"No, he wouldn't bite anyone. He just has this habit of wanting to chew a lot of stuff. He's wrecked a bunch of our baseballs and footballs. Luckily, he hasn't become interested in furniture. That would be a different kind of problem."

Andrew looked at Archie, then back at Dooley. "That's a lot of stuff going on in Archie's life. Seems like you could write a book about it. "

"Yeah, well, then things really changed. After Thanksgiving, mom wants to send Archie away. She's angry like you can't believe. It is bad. My dad, he tells Archie in their special language what's going on and Archie doesn't mess up after that. You can see, he's still here. But for a while it didn't look good for him. Then he saved my life and everything changed. "

Just then, two women and two teenage girls carrying manila folders rounded the corner from the entrance to the Cazenovia College Admissions Office and almost bumped into the boys and Archie. The girls jumped back at the sight of the huge dog and the skinny black boy. "Oh, my God, this town is so different than the brochures. That's the fifth one I've seen," one woman whispered to the other woman covering her mouth with the back of her hand. Andrew and Dooley overheard her remark.

Dooley turned to Andrew. "They won't see five dogs like Archie in Cazenovia. He's one of a kind."

Andrew's shoulders slumped as he cast his eyes toward the ground and shook his head slightly and said in a low voice, "I don't think they're talkin' about Archie."

Dooley frowned and paused before speaking. "Don't pay them any mind, Andrew. They don't live in Cazenovia. People are real nice here."

Andrew tugged on Dooley's sleeve. "You were sayin' Archie saved your life. How'd that happen?"

"Oh yeah, after Thanksgiving things were really bad around the house. Mom and dad didn't talk to each other a whole lot. We had to keep Archie away from mom. A couple of months later, Bob, Archie and I went on a Boy Scout camping trip. I fell off a footbridge into a creek that went to a steep waterfalls. The water was so cold, you wouldn't believe it! Froze me up solid, like an ice cube. Couldn't move my arms and legs to swim. I'm tellin ya, thought I was gonna die. But Archie knew something was wrong and he jumped in the water and saved me. When mom learned about it, she got all emotional. Now Archie is like her kid. He can do no wrong."

Andrew shook his head, an incredulous look crossing his face. "Dooley, they should make a movie about Archie. He like Superman and Rin-Tin-Tin together."

Dooley bent over to rub Archie's head. "Yeah, he's a pretty good dog. I probably wouldn't be here if it weren't for him."

In front of Aikman's Hardware, Archie suddenly stopped. He wouldn't budge, no matter how hard Andrew tugged the rope. "We need to keep movin', Archie, we got places to go." Archie merely lowered his head and dragged Andrew to the door of the store, and sat down.

"Oh, yeah, Andrew, you should know this. Aikman's is one of Archie's regular stops. He goes here most days on his own. The boss here, Mr. Evans, and the guy who runs the pharmacy across the street, they both treat Archie like a king. He can walk in their stores. They give him treats. Everybody in town knows Archie. He could run for mayor if he was a person."

A middle aged woman in a polka dot dress, broad brimmed straw hat and white gloves, carrying a brown handbag with the straps at her elbow, approached the front door. "Well, hello, Dooley, how are you today?" She bent over and petted Archie on the top of his head. Archie craned his neck in appreciation. "And how's the town's favorite dog?" She turned her attention to Andrew. "And I see you have some company today."

"This is Andrew, Mrs. Doyle. He's from Harlem and he's staying with us two weeks. He's gonna get some fresh air."

"I see. Well I hope you have a nice time here, Andrew. I've never been to Harlem. I'm sure you'll find it quite different here." Andrew just looked at her with a blank expression as she smiled at the boys and went into the store.

Around the corner strolled Parnell Hughes with a young black boy about Andrew's age and size. The young fellow wore a short-sleeved madras shirt buttoned to the top and khaki pants with the bottom rolled up. Andrew's eyes widened and a smile formed. "Hey, Lionel, this here's my new friend, Dooley. And this is Archie. They been showing me around town today. Dooley, Lionel and I come from the same neighborhood."

Lionel, about Andrew's age, stared at the huge dog and shielded himself behind Parnell who stepped forward, nodded at

Dooley, then started vigorously rubbing Archie's back and chest. "Here's the town hero," Parnell smiled.

Lionel stayed at a distance from the gathering then circled behind Dooley and Andrew. He approached his friend and whispered, "Andrew, I never saw no dog big as that one. He not gonna eat us, is he?"

"Lionel, I s'pose he *could* eat us if he wanted to on account of him being part wolf. But, he's my friend. And 'cause I got this rope, he knows I'm the boss today."

Lionel's eyes widened and his mouth opened in a circle. "Even the po-lice dogs we see in Harlem, they ain't this big. How come he lets you be the boss?"

"'Cause I live with him now and he's gettin' to know me, even though it's only one day. You can pet him if you want to. He's safe. He won't bite you. Even the little girls in my house here, they climb all over him. All he does is lick their faces and make them laugh."

Lionel cautiously approached Archie making sure Andrew stood between him and the dog. He bent at the waist, extending his right arm toward the huge dog. Gently, he stroked Archie's head as the dog panted, looking into Lionel's eyes. "I never petted no wolf before. Wait 'til I tell my momma."

Dooley held open the door and the group entered just as Art Evans finished stocking a shelf and turned to the four boys. "Hello fellas, come on in. I see we have some new customers today." Art smiled at the boys as he approached Archie and rubbed his head. Archie licked a familiar hand. "How's Troop 18's favorite mascot today?"

"He's good, Mr. Evans. Just showing my new friend, Andrew, around town. He and Lionel, here, they're from Harlem."

"I see. Welcome to Cazenovia, boys." Art reached out to shake each boy's hand. Lionel and Andrew each extended his hand sheepishly, unaccustomed as they were to shaking hands with white people.

Archie started pulling Andrew toward the counter at the back of the store. Andrew tried to pull Archie back but without success. The ancient floorboards creaked as the dog and boy made a hurried trip past the hand tools to the back.

Art laughed. "Looks like Archie wants his Milk Bone now. He knows just where I keep them. I think I have some lollipops back there for you boys." Moments later, Archie had his front paws on top of the four-foot high counter with his long pink tongue hanging down and his tail moving like a windmill, forcing Andrew to back away. Art distributed the treats and the boys bade him goodbye as they headed out the door, across the street and into Theobald's pharmacy. Andrew strained to hold Archie near him.

Once inside Theobald's, the same thing happened as Fred Theobald met the newcomers and gave Archie what he usually received. Afterward, the four boys walked around town and meandered the three blocks from downtown to Lakeside Park, the public swimming place. Dooley removed the rope from Archie's collar and the dog made a beeline for the water where he swam out about thirty yards.

Outside the park entrance, five boys aged about fourteen to fifteen noticed Dooley, Parnell and the visitors. They nodded to one another, patted one another on the back and approached Dooley and his friends. Andrew watched them come closer. The tallest of the group tossed aside the cigarette he was smoking. Another, with gaps in his bottom teeth and cheeks covered in acne, cracked his knuckles as he drained a can of beer wrapped in a brown paper bag. They all wore cutoff blue jean shorts with tattered edges and three had sleeveless white tee-shirts.

Dooley shook his head and turned to Parnell. "Here comes trouble." Andrew noticed this quiet exchange between Parnell and Dooley.

Lionel had discovered the tree swing swimmers used to catapult themselves into the seven-foot deep water. Even though he did not know how to swim, he held the ropes tightly as he rhythmically swung a few feet back and forth over the edge of the pier. Andrew frowned as he stood ten feet from the diving board on the pier. "Hey Dooley, those guys, they not your friends?"

"No. They go to Burton Street School on the other side of town. We play tackle football with them on the green sometimes and there's always fights. We don't like them and they don't like us. They're just a bunch of bullies."

Dooley and Parnell stood in front of Andrew as the group approached. Archie remained swimming in the shallow water playing with a few kids who had trailed him.

"Hey, O'Neill, hey Hughes, what's up with you and the monkeys? I see that one is still swingin' from the trees." The Burton Street boys chuckled and slapped one another's arms. Dooley and Parnell shook their heads and remained standing in front of Andrew, who frowned at the mention of 'monkeys' and looked around for an escape path if he needed one. Parnell put his hands on his hips and spread his feet apart in front of Andrew who stood four steps from the diving board. Lionel, meanwhile, seemed oblivious to the evolving trouble.

Dooley stepped forward. "Spencer, why don't you and your stupid friends just go home. If I remember right, you didn't make it in scouts because you couldn't swim. So, what are you doing at the lake? Taking lessons?"

"You're a jerk, O'Neill. And aren't you the one who fell into Chittenango Creek? Nice move, super scout. And now I guess you love darkies too. Cause I see a lot of them around town. They should go back to the jungle or wherever they come from."

"You know, Spencer, you're so stupid you probably can't even locate Harlem on a map. And that's where our friends come from. Know where Harlem is, Spencer?"

"Yeah, well so what, O'Neill. Who gives a crap where Harlem is? Probably just a place full of them." Spencer's friends moved slowly to the left and right of Dooley and Parnell.

"It's in New York City, stupid." Parnell stepped forward almost chest to chest with Spencer. Dooley moved an arm's length from Parnell, preparing to defend himself if one of the older boys lurched at him. "And these are our new friends. So why don't you and your band of broken toys get out of here?"

Spencer shoved Parnell, who was taller than Spencer by a head and ten pounds heavier. Parnell pushed him to the ground and jumped on Spencer as they wrestled in the grass. Two of Spencer's friends rushed past Parnell. One grabbed Dooley around the stomach as the other tackled Dooley who landed a punch to the first boy's waist. The three of them rolled in a scrum as six fists pummeled midsections. Andrew stood frozen as the two other Burton Street boys ran toward him and pushed him down.

Lionel turned his head at the commotion and screamed, "Help", drawing the attention of mothers minding their children thirty yards away in the shallow sandy area.

Billy and Joey, who had pushed Andrew, looked toward the shallow swimming area and saw women standing and pointing in their direction. "Let's get out of here," Billy shouted. He and Joey bolted toward the park entrance leaving their three friends to contend with Parnell and Dooley.

Archie, meanwhile had emerged from the shallow water, shook himself, then raced toward the commotion near the diving pier. While two Burton Street boys continued to punch Dooley in his ribs, Parnell overpowered Spencer, who was no match for the star running back of middle school. Covering the distance from the shallow water to the diving pier in six-foot strides, Archie bolted to Dooley and stopped just short of the wrestling threesome.

Pausing five feet from them, Archie bared his teeth and lowered himself on his haunches as he emitted a low, guttural, menacing growl. Freddy and Al, upon hearing these sounds, got off Dooley and started to move slowly away from him. "I seen that dog around town," Freddy said to his friend, "but I ain't never seen him growl like that."

Lionel had jumped off the swing and stood with his arms around Andrew's waist, hiding behind him. Andrew's body shook as he summoned the courage to shout out, "You guys better leave before Dooley tells Archie to eat you. He can too on account of him being part wolf. He ain't afraid of you."

Freddy and Al looked at each other with concern as they slowly stepped back twenty feet and then high-tailed it for the front gate looking back to see if Archie had followed them. Dooley gathered his wits and rushed over to pull Spencer off of Parnell. Archie trailed, still growling.

Parnell put Spencer in a head brace as Dooley held Spencer's arms behind his back. "Okay, let him go, Dooley." Parnell stood next to Dooley, both breathing heavily, as Archie stood near them, still letting out a low growl. Lionel and Andrew came up behind their friends, standing as close as possible to Archie. Parnell shoved Spencer's shoulders. "Tell your jerk friends we don't want to see you or them around here anymore. We kicked your butts in football and we'll do the same here. So, stay the heck away from us. Understand?" Parnell glowered at the boy. Spencer spat on the ground and nodded, then walked toward the entrance. He stopped to light a cigarette, looked back, held up his right hand middle finger and then disappeared down Albany Street.

Dooley broke a long silence as the boys stared at each other. "Andrew, Lionel, don't think most people in Cazenovia are like those jerks. They're the bad apples in the bushel. That's why we don't like them. They don't think like Parnell and me. We're happy you're here. We're gonna have a good time together, right Parnell?" Parnell nodded.

Andrew summoned his courage to speak. "Dooley, we got bad people like that in Harlem too. We don't pay them no mind, right Lionel?" Lionel slowly shook his head up and down. "I think so long as we have Archie near us, everything gonna be all right. Wherever I go, if I'm with Archie, I know I'm safe."

A lady approached the group. "Boys, is everything alright? I saw some fighting going on over here and then Archie looked like he was bothered."

Parnell looked at his friends. "Oh, we're fine Mrs. Ryan. Just a friendly wrestling match with some guys from Burton Street. No big deal." She nodded and returned to her children.

"Listen," Parnell continued when the woman was out of earshot, "if word gets out about this, they'll cancel the program and nobody's gonna get any more fresh air. We gotta be real. Let's keep this between us otherwise our parents will make a big deal of it and then nobody gets to come from Harlem anymore. Are we all okay with that?" Everyone nodded.

Andrew and Archie settled into a familiar routine. Bob and Dooley had baseball every morning and papers to deliver in the afternoons. While they did some activities with Andrew, at least part of everyday Archie and Andrew would wander off on their own. Passers-by who had not seen the "fresh air" visitors did a double take at the sight of a small black boy shepherding a huge dog on a tether. Andrew soon dispensed with the leash and Archie stayed close by him on their walks. He often spontaneously hugged the dog who reciprocated by licking his face. Betty gave Andrew a quarter every morning to get a treat, which usually was a strawberry ice cream cone from Allen's Variety Store.

At dinner, Archie now lay beneath the table next to Andrew instead of Patrick. Andrew had learned Patrick's tricks. When Betty turned to feed Timmer in the highchair, he discreetly shoveled broccoli or green beans into his hand and fed the unwanted vegetables to Archie.

One lazy afternoon during Andrew's second week, Betty and Timmer were on the porch while Dooley and Andrew played catch in the yard. The phone rang. "Boys, keep an eye on Timmer. I'll be back in a minute." She went inside to answer it without realizing the porch gate was open.

Moments later, Andrew missed catching a ball and both boys followed its path toward the house. They saw Archie near the end of the driveway walking back toward the porch. His jaws were clamped around a cloth diaper with a happily gurgling Timmer dangling. "Holy smokes!" Dooley exclaimed as he ran to Archie and took a wriggling Timmer from him. Dooley placed Timmer back on his blanket. Archie lay across the porch opening. Dooley stood back and watched as Timmer crawled to Archie and tried to climb on his back. The dog gently nudged the toddler back toward the blanket.

Andrew watched all this without uttering a word. Finally, he blurted out, "Archie, you a smart dog and a good babysitter too!"

Dooley went to the front door and stuck his head part way around the opening. He heard Betty on the phone. "Andrew, we're gonna keep this our little secret, okay?" Andrew nodded with a quizzical look crossing his face. "If my mom learns we almost let Timmer crawl into the street, we're gonna get in trouble."

"Your mom, she be happy Archie lookin' after him so good."

"Um, not quite. She likes Archie a lot now. But she doesn't expect him to look after Timmer. That's our job and we messed up. So, our secret, okay?"

Andrew raised his eyebrows and nodded his head slowly. "Oh, I get it. We just keep this to ourselves."

Dooley held out the pinkie of his right hand toward Andrew. "Let's pinkie shake on it, alright?"

"Yeah, we do that back home too." And the boys joined fingers.

Two days later, the boys moved about the living room filling their backpacks for a scout camping trip as Archie paced from them to the door, anticipating going with them. He shoved his big head inside a backpack and Dooley pushed him away. Betty looked up from her knitting and saw Archie at the door. "Not this time, Archie," she said.

Archie moved to Bob and nuzzled his shoulder. "No, Archie. Andrew's leaving in a couple of days, you get to stay here with him."

The next morning the boys helped each other adjust their backpacks then hugged Betty before starting down Green Street toward the scout lodge. Archie slinked off the porch unnoticed, went around the back of the house then bolted after them. Andrew and Patrick were drinking lemonade on the porch when they saw Archie halfway down the block. Andrew leaped off the porch, ran as fast as he could and caught up with Archie as Dooley and Bob stood in the street pointing for Archie to return home. Andrew grabbed the dog by the collar. "Archie, Archie, you not invited on this trip. You stay with me."

Bob and Dooley yelled at Archie to stay behind. Andrew used all his strength to hold the dog. Archie looked first at the boys, then back at Andrew. He started to whine. The appearance of backpacks had always signaled to him a trip with the boys. Andrew struggled to hold the dog, digging his heels into the pavement. But Archie's weight advantage caused Andrew's sneakers to slide along the street as he continued to lose this battle. After almost two blocks, and with the boys out of sight, Archie stopped pulling and shoved his giant muzzle into Andrew's hands and licking them. They walked side by side back home.

Andrew petted Archie's head. "Good boy, Archie, you stay with me. You and I go for our walk later."

That afternoon Andrew and Archie wandered into town for their strawberry ice cream cone. With Archie lying at his side, Andrew sat on a corner bench in Veteran's Park with bushes shielding them from passers-by on Albany Street. Spencer and Joey from the Burton Street gang spotted them.

Andrew noticed the boys whispering to each other then slapping one another on their backs. They walked toward the bench. "I see you're still here, huh, darkie? Isn't it time you go back to, where is that, Harlem?"

Andrew said nothing.

"Can't you hear, boy? I asked you a question. Time to go home, right?"

Andrew continued sitting, licking his ice cream with Archie next to him. "You guys are the bad apples. That's the way I see it."

Both boys shook their heads. "So, we're bad apples." Spencer puffed out his chest and stepped forward. "What you gonna do about that?"

"Yeah," Joey added, standing behind Spencer as he eyed Archie cautiously.

Andrew shrugged, focusing on his cone. "I don't got to do nuthin'. I got Archie. So long as he's with me, I feel real safe."

Spencer walked within five feet of Andrew. Archie emitted a low, guttural growl. Spencer halted then stuck out his chin and gestured toward Archie.

"I seen this dog around town. He don't worry me. You know, I've been hankering for a strawberry ice cream cone. Why don't you give me that one?" Spencer raised his arm quickly trying to snatch the cone. Archie leaped toward the boy, his front legs hitting Spencer square in the shoulders forcing the boy to fall onto his back on the grass. Archie straddled the boy, his massive head inches from Spencer. Spencer covered his face with his hands. As Archie growled in a low tone, Andrew remained on the bench licking his ice cream.

Joey ran from the scene as fast as he could while Andrew looked at Spencer. "Did anybody tell you Archie is half wolf? 'Cause that's true. His daddy was a wild wolf. Now he's my protector, wherever I go." Spencer turned white as a ghost. "I think if you was to apologize to me, Archie would like that. He also won't eat you if I tell him not to 'cause he'd rather eat this here cone."

Spencer groaned. "Look, I'm sorry already. Nobody told me he was a wolfdog."

Andrew stood, called Archie to follow him and the dog responded immediately. Spencer got up and bolted after Joey who was a block away. Andrew finished the ice cream and gave Archie the cone. They walked home.

The following afternoon, Betty and the kids planned to head to the lake to escape the heat. Andrew approached Betty in the den where she was knitting a Christmas stocking.

"Mrs. 'Neill, you sure do knit a lot of them stockin's. Who you givin' that one to?"

"Well, Andrew, if you promise to keep a secret, I'll tell you. It's for Archie. Everyone else in the family has one. I just thought he might like one too. What do you think?"

Oh, that's a great idea, Mrs. 'Neill. Santa Claus, he prob'ly bring Archie lots of presents, like good bones for chewin', him being special and all. You know, I was thinkin', is it okay if him and me stay here? We could hang out on the porch together. He likes it there. It's nice and cool. And I like having time with just the two of us."

"Andrew, that's a good idea. I know you and Archie will be fine here. We'll be back in a little while. Oh, you know what? I just picked up some juicy apples at the store. I'll wash some off and leave them in a bowl on the kitchen table." Archie and Andrew sat in the shade on the porch as the boy devoured a large red apple, biting off chunks and sharing them with Archie.

Andrew looked in the dog's eyes and placed his right arm around Archie's back as he handed him an apple chunk with his other hand. "You know, Archie, I be goin' home soon. I wish you could come with me. You'd like Harlem, only we don't have no lakes there. We got a lot of concrete. But there's some parks where we could walk. And they got strawberry ice cream cones, just like here. Maybe you could come for a visit." Archie licked apple juice drops from Andrew's chin as the boy laughed.

Bob and Dooley returned the following day from camping. Betty made a farewell dinner for Andrew, using Aunty Anne's special pot-roast recipe. Archie stationed himself in his usual spot under the kitchen table and received his customary ration of unwanted delicacies.

"That sure was a good dinner, Mrs. 'Neill." Andrew rubbed his stomach and smiled. "Hard to believe I got to go home tomorrow. Sure has been fun being in this family. But I'll be glad to see my momma and grand mom."

Betty smiled and placed a reassuring hand on Andrew's shoulder and rubbed it gently. "Maybe we can have you back next year. What do you think kids?" The older boys nodded and the Irish twins squealed and clapped their hands. Archie appeared from under the table and his ears perked at the sudden commotion.

Bob and Dooley cleaned up the kitchen as Andrew, Patrick and Archie headed to the porch. Betty took the three younger kids upstairs for a bath. The sun appeared low on the horizon and a soft breeze blew the American flag angled on its pole near the front door. The boys rocked gently in chairs, silently enjoying each other's company as Archie sprawled across the floor.

Andrew was not looking forward to departure day. While he wanted to see his family back in Harlem, he had grown accustomed to the rhythm of life with his new family. Just when he was feeling like "one of the gang", it was time to go. The kids finished their pancake breakfast, Andrew's favorite, and washed up. Betty motioned to all of them as they milled about the kitchen. "Come on, kids, everybody in the car. The bus is taking off at nine. Bob, put Andrew's suitcase in the far back with Archie." Archie jumped in the back of the station wagon. They left the tailgate window down so he could stick out his head. The family drove back to the school where the Harlem bus awaited them.

Andrew sat in the back seat between Dooley and Patrick with Maureen laughing and fidgeting on his lap. Lisa sat on Dooley's lap. Bob held Timmer in the front. "I sure am gonna miss Cazenovia," Andrew said. "Archie and me, we walked every one of these streets, didn't we Archie?" He turned to rub the dog's head. They pulled into the school parking lot as groups of white families piled out of cars with a black boy or girl. The Harlem children greeted their traveling companions as they brought suitcases to the bus driver to load in the storage compartment. Most of the children appeared happy, in stark contrast to three weeks earlier when they had emerged from the bus with worried faces showing fear of the unknown. Small black children now hugged larger white women with tears of happiness.

Betty stood in front of her children and knelt down to hug Andrew. "Andrew, you'll always be a part of our family and Cazenovia will always be your second home. I hope you can come back next summer and we'll work on improving your swimming. Maybe we'll even go on a sailboat. You know, you'll have to send us a picture of your family. Here's one of our family with our address printed on the back."

"You have Archie in the middle of this picture," Andrew smiled. "I'm gonna tell everybody on my block about him and you."

Andrew put both arms around Betty's neck and buried his head in her shoulders. He felt his eyes start to get moist. He withdrew from Betty, rubbed his eyes with his palms then shook hands with Bob who held a squirming Timmer. Andrew rubbed the toddler's head. "Timmer, you gonna be a big guy when I see you next summer." The toddler laughed and held out his hands toward Andrew who took him from Bob and held the boy in the air.

The Irish twins squealed as they ran towards Andrew and each grabbed one of his legs. He handed Timmer back to Bob then bent over and hugged the girls as he placed his head between theirs. As the girls let go, Patrick, six inches shorter than Andrew, approached him and gently hugged Andrew around his waist. Then he looked into Andrew's hazel eyes. "I didn't know I was going to like you so much. Now, I'm going to miss the stories we tell in bed. I want you to come back so you can tell us more about how you live in the big city."

"I will, Patrick." Then Andrew enveloped him as he bent over to whisper to Patrick. "Make sure you remember our trick about givin' Archie them vegetables when your mom not watchin' us, right?" Patrick nodded and smiled.

Andrew turned to Dooley who first shook his hand then encircled Andrew in a bear hug. Andrew stood back and placed his hands on Dooley's shoulders, looking him squarely in the eyes. "We like brothers now, you and me. I'm Andrew Michael and you Michael Andrew. We share the same name only backwards and frontwards. How'd our mamas know to do that?" They bent over at the waist and laughed.

Dooley raised his index finger. "Hey, I got you something you can use with your friends back home, now that you're a star player." Dooley ran to the car and from under a blanket in the far back brought out a bag and handed it to Andrew.

He opened the bag and his eyes widened to the size of quarters as a smile covered his face. "It's a Mickey Mantle. I never owned a baseball glove. It's nice and soft too. This must have cost you a lot of money."

"That's okay. I just mowed a few more lawns and got lucky on my paper route tips. And Bob gave me an advance on my share for next week. So, while I'm delivering papers to pay off that glove, I'll be thinking about you enjoying it with your friends. They got baseball fields in Harlem, right?"

"Oh yeah, we walk over to Central Park. They got plenty o' fields there."

Dooley smiled. "Good. And I rubbed neat's-foot oil all over it to make it limber. Here, keep this ball with it. At night, put it under your pillow with the ball in the pocket and it'll get nice and loose. When you come back next summer, make sure you bring it 'cause we're gonna need you at shortstop." Andrew grinned as he tried on the glove and threw the baseball a few times into the webbing.

Finally, the Harlem-bound boy turned to Archie. He knelt and wrapped his arms around the dog's neck as tears involuntarily streamed down his cheeks. "I never forget you, Archie," he whispered in the dog's ear. "You made my life so good here." Andrew hugged him even harder as the tears flowed down his cheeks and over his chin. Archie licked the boy's face. Andrew and Archie seemed as though they were alone on a stage under a spotlight. "Ain't no one in Harlem never had a wolfdog for a best friend, but now I do."

Betty addressed Andrew as she smiled at her children. "Andrew, do you remember when you and Archie first met? Could you believe now what you thought then, that you and he would be such good friends?"

Andrew rose from a crouch near Archie and placed his hands under the dog's jaw, holding the dog's gaze. "I remember how scared I was when you jumped on my shoulders, Archie. Now I wish I could take you on this bus with me. You taught me what it's like to be extra special and feel safe. I never knowed a dog like you in my life." He held the photo in front of Archie. "I'll keep this picture taped to the wall near my bed so I can see you every night."

Archie withdrew from Andrew and licked the boy's hands gently. Andrew hugged him once more. Finally, the bus driver yelled "all aboard". Andrew caressed Archie's head as he pulled away from the wolfdog and mounted the steps. Moments later the bus pulled away. Archie sat looking at the bus as it drove into the distance. Andrew waved out the window, his eyes trained on Archie until the dog was out of sight.

15.   School Days

The latest Beatles' hit blared from the transistor radio as Bob and Dooley brushed their teeth in the only bathroom at One Union Street. Bob wiped his mouth on a towel and turned to Dooley. "We got to eat breakfast fast. The seniors have a practice drill for graduation at 8:30 and I can't be late. You have to get the kids ready 'cause Mom has to be at the college early." Dooley nodded as he spit out a white slur and cupped his hand and head under the running faucet.

"Yeah, okay," Dooley gurgled. "I hope Lisa is moving. I don't need another detention slip on account of her."

"Well, I can't worry about that. She's your problem."

Dooley grabbed the towel from his brother as he turned off the radio. "Hey, by the way, I finally told Mr. Ryan that Eddie's taking over the paper route since Patrick won't, and I start at Montgomery Ward tomorrow. Archie won't know what to do with his afternoons!"

Bob looked at Dooley and shrugged with his palms held upward. "He'll just have more time for cruising around town or just hanging on the porch. You see how it takes him longer to get up from lying down. He's getting old. Hurry up. We have to keep moving."

The boys hoofed it to the kitchen where Betty flopped French toast on plates as she gave them a slight frown. "It's about time, you two. I have to leave in a few minutes. Dooley, remember, you're in charge of the girls. C'mon Timmer, we have to get you to Mrs. Arnold's. Boys, there's French toast on the stove for you." She grabbed Timmer from a booster seat and headed for the door turning her head sideways. "Everybody, be good. And don't knock over those moving boxes in the living room. We have to make sure all the packing is done by the end of the month."

Archie sat on the kitchen floor turning his head toward whoever was speaking. Bob had fed him earlier that morning and let him out for his morning constitutional in the field behind Fiedler's garage. Lisa poured a huge amount of maple syrup on her toast while Bob and Dooley wolfed down their breakfast.

Dooley grabbed the container from her. "Whoa, Lisa, you think you have enough syrup? You could sink a ship with that much."

Lisa dipped her index finger in the pool she had created. "I like the syrup more than the toast. It's yummy."

"Well, start eating," Dooley replied with a furrowed brow as he checked the kitchen clock. Maureen and Patrick ate contentedly while Bob finished his breakfast, grabbed his books and headed for the door.

"You're on your own, Dooley. See you later."

Maureen looked at Dooley. "I'm full and my hands are icky."

Dooley grabbed a dishcloth, cleaned his sister's hands and mouth, then gave Archie the remnants of her breakfast, which he ate lying down. Surveying the kitchen table, he barked out orders. "All right, we are out of here in ten minutes. Patrick, you put the dishes in the dishwasher and wipe the table. Girls, you come with me; I have to braid your hair. Who knows where the rubber bands are?" Dooley and the girls proceeded to the den where he found rubber bands.

Lisa, now eight, told Dooley she had to go to the bathroom and would follow in a few minutes. He looked at her with a quizzical expression. "Okay, do what you need to do and get moving. Patrick and Maureen, you're coming with me."

By now Archie had moved outside to the porch, waiting to walk with the kids to school. Dooley bolted through the open front door with the broken knob that never allowed it to shut tightly and pushed the warped screen door open with Patrick and Maureen following. "Archie, you stay here and come with Lisa." Archie rose slowly, approached the screen door, used his left paw to pull it open at a curve in the frame, pushed the wooden door open with his snout and walked inside.

Lisa didn't actually need to use the bathroom. She stood at the window with Archie watching the others round the corner. She wanted to be just late enough to avoid her least favorite duty, delivering milk to the classrooms at break. And that meant figuring out another excuse that would spare her from detention.

As a matter of record if a student was tardy, he or she reported to the principal's office to explain the reason and get a late slip for the teacher. Lisa had become an expert in the lateness drill. Holes in her sock, a forgotten book that required retrieving, a misplaced homework assignment, an alarm clock that ran out of batteries, you name it, she invented it. However, she was running out of good reasons. Two more weak excuses and she'd enjoy the company of others in detention after school, doing math problems while the sound of laughter from the playground wafted in through the windows.

She scanned the room as she scratched her head. Archie came and sat in front of her and placed his paw on her leg. "Archie, you're waiting for me, aren't you, good boy?" Archie licked her leg as she rubbed his head. "Okay, I'm coming, I gotta figure out just one more thing." She looked around the downstairs then put her finger to her lip and then suddenly grinned. She placed one Buster Brown loafer on her left foot, deliberately leaving its mate on the floor. She grabbed her books that were held together by a thick elastic band and with Archie trailing, walked through the open front door leaving it that way and held the screen door for Archie. She limped toward the shortcut to school, her shoeless sock collecting dirt.

They cut through Anderson's back yard, across the street from their house and bordering the school. Archie trailed Lisa with his head bobbing up and down following Lisa's uneven gait. They went through the well-worn hole in the chain link fence that surrounded the school and approached the front entrance.

"Archie, I'll see you at lunch time." Lisa vigorously petted his head. Archie proceeded to the carpet remnant next to the front door where he remained every day school was in session. He slurped water from the bowl next to the carpet and sat upright as he watched Lisa through the glass partition walk into the principal's office located immediately inside. The secretary watched Lisa approach, looked at the clock on the wall and shook her head.

"You're ten minutes late, miss. What's your excuse today?"

"Oh, hi, Mrs. Crandall. I couldn't find my other shoe. See?" Lisa pointed at her foot.

"Where do you think it might be, Lisa?"

"I don't know. I looked everywhere. I just came like this 'cause I didn't want to be too late. I figure I'll find it at lunchtime."

"Very, well, Lisa. We'll just count this as an excused tardiness. Make sure you come back from lunch hour wearing two shoes." Lisa smiled like a Cheshire cat. Phyllis Crandall signed a small yellow slip of paper and handed it to her.

Just then, a young girl nine or ten years old stepped to a microphone in the office. "May I have your attention. Please rise for the Pledge of Allegiance." She recited it as Lisa and others in the office stood at attention with their right hands over their hearts. When she was done, she took a water pitcher outside to fill Archie's bowl. She looked around but Archie was not in his usual place.

Lisa limped down the hall toward her classroom. Two classmates, each carrying one side of a crate filled with pint sized bottles of white and chocolate milk, rounded the corner and almost bumped into her. Joan Muldoon frowned. "Lisa, you missed your turn for milk duty again so Mrs. Rayburn made me do it." Joan looked down at Lisa's feet. "And how come you only got one shoe?"

"On account of I couldn't find the other one. Why else would I wear only one? But I'm not getting in trouble for it." Lisa held her chin high.

Inside the class, Mrs. Rayburn discussed the Spanish conquest of the Americas. As Lisa hobbled into the room, the class erupted in gales of laughter. Lisa's face turned red and with her back to the class facing the teacher she blurted out, "What the heck, hasn't everyone seen a person wearing just one shoe before?"

She turned around to face the class and looked up to where everyone else had turned their heads. On the opposite wall, sitting in front of the glass door to the ground level exit used for fire drills, stood Archie, ears upright, wagging his tail and looking into the classroom. He had a Buster Brown penny loafer in his mouth.

***

Graduation morning arrived to perfect weather. The high school band's preparations traveled through the air the quarter mile to the house. "Bob, you go ahead since you have to be there first." Betty walked to the bottom of the stairs. "Kids, I laid out the clothes I want you to wear. Dooley, help Timmer with his suspenders."

As Bob headed toward the door, he turned. "What about Dad, Mom? He's coming, right?"

"Yes, he'll be there. He's bringing your grandmother."

"I sure wish Grandpa and Grandma Hesburgh could be here," Bob said wistfully.

Betty straightened out the lapel on Bob's navy blazer. He wore gray slacks, shiny black penny loafers, a crisp white shirt and a bright red tie. Tears of joy welled up in her as she admired how handsome her eighteen year-old son had become. Then she hugged him.

"Grandpa will be with you in spirit today, sweetheart, and we'll see Grandma tomorrow at Loretta Rest. Everyone's very proud of you, the first O'Neill graduate!"

"You're bringing Archie, right?" Bob asked. "It's like he's graduating too."

"Of course, he'll be there, won't you Archie?" At the mention of his name, Archie labored off the living room rug and approached them. Betty petted his head. Archie craned his neck in a circular motion and stretched his entire body.

Betty turned to face upstairs. "C'mon, kids. We have to leave in fifteen minutes. Everyone come down so I can check on you."

Betty wore a navy dress with red polka dots, black pumps and white gloves. The girls, now ten and eleven, wore matching pink dresses they had picked out with Betty at J.C. Penney's Department Store. They were normally worn only for Sunday school, but today was an exception.

Dooley tugged at the collar of his white shirt while playing with the knot of a solid blue tie. He carried a madras sport coat over his arm. Betty straightened his tie. "Dooley, you can put your coat on when we get there. You look very handsome. The best lookin' almost 16-year old boy!"

Patrick followed Dooley downstairs, his blue shirt half untucked from khaki pants, as he fiddled with a red clip-on bowtie. Rolled in a ball he carried a royal blue blazer. Betty approached him and took the blazer out of his hands. "Patrick, see how Dooley has his coat folded? Carry yours like that too, not rolled in a ball like dirty laundry. You're thirteen. I know you can do better. Okay?"

Six year-old Timmer trailed his brothers wearing plaid shorts with red suspenders over an ivory colored short-sleeve shirt. Betty straightened out his suspenders. "Now there's a good looking fella," she smiled.

The family headed out the door to walk the three blocks to the field in front of the high school. Betty greeted her neighbors, Charlie and Evie Gregg, whose daughter, Patty, was graduating with Bob. The three adults laughed as they shared some pleasant memories of their eldest children finishing the first chapters of their lives.

Betty smiled at Charlie. "That was quite a rendition of reveille you played at six this morning. Better than most days. But I think you need to work on your version of 'Pomp and Circumstance'. If the neighborhood didn't know what was happening today, they probably have a clue now!" Charlie and Evie laughed as the group rounded the corner toward the school.

As the Cazenovia High School Marching Band played 'America the Beautiful', seats filled in front of an empty stage awaiting the graduates. Dooley turned to his mother. "Mom, look, there's Dad with grandma."

"Go say hi to them, Dooley."

Dooley and Patrick followed Archie who had moved slowly to Big Bob's side on seeing him. Archie's tail moved in whirlwind fashion as he approached Big Bob and Bob's mother. Archie rubbed his snout against the man's leg. Bob, who wore a slate gray suit, white shirt and blue tie, leaned over to cup his hands around Archie's face. "Great wolfdog, you are becoming gray like me, and you are looking more distinguished than ever." The dog retreated slightly and licked Bob's hands.

Bob's eighty-five year old mother wore a drab solid blue dress. She accompanied it with a gray hat cocked to one side with a protruding feather. She petted Archie's head once. Dooley whispered to Patrick, "Grandma looks like an old version of Robin Hood's girlfriend." Patrick put his hand to his mouth suppressing a laugh. The boys hugged their father and gave their grandmother a hurried embrace. Bob's mother avoided eye contact with Betty and stiffly smiled at her grandsons.

The girls and Timmer hugged their father and gave a perfunctory embrace to their grandmother, who patted their heads with a gray gloved hand. They quickly returned to Betty's side.

Dooley made small talk with his father and grandmother. Patrick remained quiet and inched his way toward Betty where he joined the Irish Twins and Timmer. Betty and Bob stood ten feet apart, glancing at each other then turning away. Dooley took his father aside for a moment. "Dad, I don't know if Mom told you yet but it looks like we're leaving Cazenovia."

"Yes, she told me a while ago a move was likely, once her night school finished and she got an offer for a guidance counsellor job. I recall she said it was Norwich where you were moving. What do you think about that?"

"Yeah, it's not real far away, maybe forty minutes. Can't say I'm real keen on moving. All my friends are here. I even went on two dates with a girl and she says I could be her boyfriend. Well, doesn't look like that's gonna happen."

Big Bob looked at his second oldest child and smiled as he put his arm around Dooley's shoulders. "You know, Dooley, life is full of surprises. You'll make new friends and there's probably another girl in Norwich who might take a fancy to a handsome devil like you."

Dooley's face turned red. "You really think so, Dad?"

"Absolutely. Good men are hard to find." Dooley looked down at his feet as his father rustled his flattop.

"Yeah, but I worry about Archie too. He doesn't know anyplace but Cazenovia. Everybody here treats him like part of their family. Every kid in this school knows him since they see him sitting at the front door every day when they arrive. I doubt that's gonna happen in Norwich. The people there probably will be scared of him once they learn he's part wolf."

"Archie will be okay. He's a survivor. Aren't you Archie?" On hearing his name, Archie's ears perked up and he rose from the grass where he'd been lying nearby. The dog approached Bob and sat facing him as he raised his right paw and stroked his master's leg.

Betty counted her children like a mother hen, got Patrick, the girls and Timmer in their seats, then looked down the end of the row where Dooley was talking with his father. She caught Dooley's eye and signaled for him to come, pointing to the stage where the graduates began to take their places. Dooley held up his right index finger and nodded to Betty.

Big Bob crouched down to eye level with Archie, cupping the dog's head in his hands. "Great wolfdog, I think we are coming to the end of our journey. I may not see you so often. Look after our small ones, like you've always done." Archie licked Bob's hand and craned his neck as Bob stroked the top of his head.

"Archie's got grey hair like you, Dad. I guess in people years he must be pretty close to your age. I know it takes him longer to go up and down the stairs."

Bob rose and remained holding Archie's gaze. "Yes, our friend is growing old. His body is aging but his mind is young." Archie raised his right paw and moved it slowly along Bob's shin. Bob closed his eyes, absorbing the touch. He cleared his throat, turning to Dooley, "Do you remember when you and I met Archie?"

"Oh yeah, I'll never forget that day. You and Mr. Greene and I walked in that room where he kept Archie. It was like Mr. Greene and I weren't even there. Archie went right up to you and stuck his nose through the wire and started licking your hand. Like he always knew you."

"The great wolfdog and I have our own language. Don't we, Archie?" Sitting, facing Bob, the dog whined, moved his head excitedly and pawed Bob's leg.

Betty called down the row, "Dooley, come on, they're almost ready to start."

"One more minute, Mom."

Bob knelt on the grass with his right knee. Placing his head next to Archie's, he rubbed the dog's body firmly with both hands.

Archie stretched, craning his neck and licked Bob's face as Dooley watched. "Dooley, do you remember old Archie Greene saying we were getting a one-of-a-kind, the only survivor in the litter, a dog to make the whole family happy?"

"He was right. I can't imagine how our lives would have been without Archie. I know I probably wouldn't be here if it weren't for him."

Bob cleared his throat again. His brow furrowed as he took a white handkerchief from his back pocket. He wiped the tiny beads of sweat forming on his hairline. His eyes welled up and a few teardrops trickled down his cheeks. "We had many good times, good friend. Like Dooley, you also helped me out of a tough situation."

Dooley frowned. "How's that, Dad? What did Archie do for you?"

"It's not important now, Dooley. Something a long time ago when our friend bailed me out of a difficult moment. Let's say he's done a lot of good for a lot of people."

Bob paused and Dooley looked sympathetically at his father. Bob rubbed his eyes again. Dooley put his hand on his father's shoulder. "It's okay, Dad, Archie understands. He knows you love him."

Bob, sighing, turned to Dooley and then to Archie. "And here we are, nine years later." He stared at the dog as several seconds passed.

Dooley squeezed his father's shoulders. "You'll see Archie again, Dad. I mean, when you come to see us, right?"

Bob looked at his son and smiled. "That's right, Dooley. You go ahead and find your seat. I don't want you getting in trouble with your mother." Dooley quickly hugged his father then moved to the other end of the aisle.

Bob turned back to Archie, standing above him as the huge dog sat at his feet, Archie's head almost reaching Bob's waist. For several seconds Bob stared at him silently. Then, bending over, caressing Archie's head, he whispered in the dog's ear, "My best decision was bringing you home that Christmas Eve." Bob massaged Archie's ears. "Goodbye, my friend. Now, go find Dooley." Bob took his seat next to his mother as Archie, looking back at Bob momentarily, moved to the other end of the row.

The seven O'Neills and Bob's mother took an entire row with Bob seated at one end and Betty at the other, bookends that did not match. Archie sat in the grass next to Betty.

After Principal Schumard had given remarks and distributed diplomas to 95 graduates, he paused. "I have one more duty to perform before we close today. One member of this class has never missed a day of school. Through rain, snow, sickness—if he had any—through all circumstances, he has remained our constant companion. Every student in this school knows his name. He has been a special member of this community. Years ago, he even saved the life of one of his family."

The audience stirred, and a faint murmuring spread among the seats.

"You have seen him walking about downtown and swimming in the lake. He has delivered some of your newspapers. He has greeted those of you who attend St. James on Sundays. He is a revered member of the local scout troop. His family, you likely have learned, is moving this summer to Norwich so you'll no longer be greeted by a familiar face at our front door. I imagine the only party happy to see him go is the Cazenovia College tennis team that fell victim to his ball-hawking ways." A ripple of laughter rose up among the audience.

Schumard nodded to young Bob who rose from his seat on stage and whistled for Archie. The big dog rose slowly and walked across the grass to the edge of the stage. Bob crouched to speak softly to Archie, whose head was almost level with the stage. He scratched behind Archie's ears as the dog moved his head from side to side. "Archie, go see Mr. Schumard."

Archie mounted the stage steps painfully and walked slowly to Schumard. Archie and Schumard knew each other well after almost eight years of the dog standing sentinel outside the principal's office. "Archie, please sit." The dog sat facing the crowd moving his head from side to side, peering first at young Bob, then at Betty and the kids, then at Big Bob. With his back to the audience Schumard faced Archie, then untied the baby blue ribbon from a diploma and unrolled it before turning to face the gathering.

"Archie O'Neill, Cazenovia High School confers on you an award for perfect attendance. For the past eight years you have greeted each student, teacher and employee who has entered our school. The elements never impeded you and you welcomed each person with consummate friendliness. You invited newcomers to our school and made them feel at home. You have been a credit to this institution. We confer upon you all rights and privileges of a graduate. Congratulations." Schumard rolled the diploma, retied the ribbon around it and placed it in Archie's mouth.

Archie extended his right paw as Schumard shook it. The audience rose in unison and applauded. They remained standing for over two minutes. Young Bob and Dooley caught each other's eyes and smiled. Dooley nudged Betty with a gleam in his eye and she smiled broadly. Patrick and the Irish Twins clapped as though they would never stop. Timmer looked at his family and joined in the applause. Big Bob swallowed hard then smiled, before nodding to himself.

Archie sat on the stage clutching the diploma in his mouth. He tilted his head left and right. Finally, he looked left and saw young Bob signaling for him to come. The new graduate embraced Archie and kissed the top of his head before telling him to go to Betty. Archie looked at the throng, then with a slight energetic spring in his step turned and walked off the stage.

16.   Last Days

Betty and her six children stood in a circle around Archie who trembled as he lay on his side on the examining room table. "He's got hip dysplasia, common in dogs this size and age, his eyes show signs of glaucoma and he probably hears poorly. That's why you have to shout to get his attention." The veterinarian pursed his lips and slightly raised his eyebrows. "How's he eating? According to my records, he appears to have lost twenty pounds since I saw him eight months back."

"That's right, Dick," Betty replied, her head shaking slightly. "He doesn't move around as much as he did even a year ago and usually doesn't eat all the food in his bowl." Twelve young eyes followed this conversation with furrowed brows.

"Look, I won't sugar coat this," the vet continued holding his palms upward. "Archie's an old dog, almost 85 in our years. You mentioned he got roughed up when he disappeared as a pup so who knows what permanent damage that caused. Just try to keep him comfortable. Limit the walks, no stairs and make sure he drinks plenty of water."

As Bob and Dooley lifted Archie from the table, Dr. Hosbach took Betty aside and whispered to her, "Betty, look, I don't want to upset your kids. Archie doesn't have a lot of time left. There's not much more I can do for him."

Outside, the dog walked gingerly to the station wagon, turning his head to the boys, waiting for them to lift him into the far back where piled blankets created a soft bed. They drove toward home in an unusual silence for six kids in close quarters. Finally, Betty broke the tense silence.

"Kids, none of us want Archie to go. Remember when Grandpa Hesburgh got old and then grew weaker. Grandpa was about the same age as Archie is now when he passed away. We'll do our best to keep Archie comfortable. How about I make meatloaf? You know he loves it." The kids numbly nodded.

Timmer turned in the back seat to stroke Archie's head. "How long is Archie gonna live, Mom?"

"I don't know, sweetheart. Only God knows."

Lisa chimed in. "I think Archie will go right to dog heaven. He only did a couple of things wrong his whole life."

"Yeah," Maureen continued, "God will give him a lot of credit for saving Dooley. Probably make him a special dog angel."

Betty turned the corner and into their driveway. "I'm sure God has good plans for Archie. He's been a special boy all his life."

Bob and Dooley lifted Archie from the car. He slowly moved to the back yard to water a shrub before lying on the small patch of lawn bordering a street used by delivery trucks going to and from the textile mill.

Since arriving in Norwich three years ago, Archie stayed close to home and the entire family went through a big transition. The town was three times the size of Cazenovia with a lot more traffic and less green space. The huge textile factory sat right in the center of the city, just three blocks from the house Betty could afford to rent. Like their home in Cazenovia, as Betty would say, it was a place best seen by candle light.

Later that day as Betty prepared dinner, Dooley went to the front porch. "Archie!" he shouted at the top of his lungs. "Dinner time, c'mon Archie." He put his hand over his eyebrows to shade the late afternoon sun as he scanned in all directions for Archie. Putting both hands to his mouth to form a megaphone, he yelled Archie's name one more time.

Across the street, an elderly Italian woman who spoke little English lived alone. She kept to herself and never interacted with the O'Neills. Betty had heard from someone at the bank that the lady's husband recently had passed away after forty years working in the textile mill. As Dooley continued shouting, he watched the lady lumber out her front door on to the porch and shake her fist at him, shouting something in Italian. Dooley scratched his head and walked around to the back of the house where he found Archie and led him inside.

Betty was setting the table. "Mom, how come that old lady across the street yelled me again in Italian? What's her problem? All I'm doing is calling Archie."

"Well, Dooley, maybe we ought to stop shouting for Archie and just go outside and find him quietly."

"So what's that got to do with her shouting at me?"

"I think she's confused, dear. She probably thinks you're calling for her. I learned from Homer Sands down at the bank that her name is Mrs. Archie." Dooley raised his eyebrows as his mouth formed an oval.

"Okay, I get it," he said. He helped Betty finish setting the table and called his brothers and sisters to come.

Cazenovia was like a Norman Rockwell painting. Everything appeared quaint and quietly happy. People on the street greeted the O'Neill kids with smiles and polite conversation and everyone seemed to know Archie and would stop to pet him. Norwich, on the other hand, was cold and impersonal. Archie seemed hesitant to wander far from home so with young Bob off at college, Dooley or Patrick would walk Archie about town to get him accustomed to his new surroundings. Typically, when they did so, people stepped back, barking cautions like, "You ought to keep that dog on a leash" or "He's not going to bite me, is he?" Rarely did anyone seek to pet him. They just tried to steer clear of him.

"He's a really friendly dog, you want to pet him?" Dooley or Patrick would say to people on the sidewalks who walked out of their way to avoid coming near to Archie.

"You just keep him under control. He looks like a wolf as much as a dog. Keep him away from me." These were the usual responses. The kids resorted to walking Archie on a leash, something the dog had not experienced in several years since Andrew from New York City first walked with Archie.

Steadily, Archie slowed down. Getting up from a lying position took him longer than it did when he lived in Cazenovia. He ate his breakfast and dinner more deliberately and sometimes didn't finish it. Some mornings he limped down the porch stairs to go to the bushes behind the house to relieve himself. His eyes became glossier, like there was a film of milk covering them. During one walk with Dooley and Patrick, a squirrel raced in front of his path and Archie did not flinch. The boys paused to look at each other. "What is it about this stupid town?" Patrick asked Dooley. "That squirrel would be a goner if we were walking down Sullivan Street in Cazenovia. Now, Archie doesn't even care about chasing them. This place is cursing Archie. He's not having any fun here."

Dooley grimaced. "Yeah, I know. You can tell he doesn't like it here. It's like he was put in prison all of a sudden. And you know how the air stinks? Not fresh like Cazenovia. I bet it's having a bad effect on Archie. He breathes that bad air and it probably just makes him have less energy. He hates it here and I do too."

While moving slower, Archie also slept most of the day. He ventured down one block to the Norwich High School athletic fields but never the five blocks into the main part of town. His past daily routine bore no resemblance to his current one. No paper route, no high school at which to stand sentry, no lake to visit for cool drinks and swims in good weather, no stores with friendly employees who gave him treats, no tennis courts to hide behind hedges to steal errant balls.

Where Cazenovia had served for nine years as a playground to a canine Marco Polo, Norwich represented a retirement home. At night, he slept downstairs in the den, no longer able to negotiate the steep staircase.

During dinner, Archie ate delicately, not finishing the meal, then lowered himself onto a blanket in the corner of the kitchen next to Betty, closing his eyes intermittently.

"I think Archie enjoyed those leftovers, Mom," Maureen, said, smiling.

"I'm sure he did," Betty replied. "But I still think her prefers turkey." Everyone laughed and Betty gave a false frown, then smiled.

"Well, that's funny now but at the time I sure didn't think it was. Archie's come a long way since then." Betty reached down to pet his head. "Now, he's a very good boy, aren't you, Archie?" The dog wagged his tail slowly making no effort to rise.

The stories of Archie continued while they cleaned up after dinner. Archie remained sleeping. The next morning, a sunny July day with the temperature approaching seventy, Bob let Archie out for his usual constitutional. A little later, as the kids began to file into the kitchen for breakfast, Dooley asked, "Anybody seen Archie?" They all rose simultaneously and went to the porch. There on the small patch of front lawn, Archie lay almost motionless except for the slow heaving of his chest.

"Mom, we gotta take Archie to the vet fast," Bob shouted upstairs. The boys gently picked him up and placed him on the blankets in the back of the station wagon. Bob got behind the wheel. Betty and Patrick joined him up front. The other four kids knelt on the back seat as eight hands stroked Archie.

Lisa and Maureen cried as they gently petted the heavily breathing dog. "Hang on, Archie. We'll be at the doctor's soon.

He'll give you some medicine to make you feel better," Lisa said as tears dripped down her cheeks onto Archie's back.

Timmer rubbed Archie's ears. "I'm gonna get you one of your favorite bones when we get home, Archie."

"You'll be okay, boy. Just stay awake," Dooley pleaded as he tried to hold back tears. "We can go for a nice walk around the block when we get home." Betty, Bob and Patrick remained silent.

Dr. Hosbach took one look at Archie and told the boys to carry him into a large cage in the back away from the barking of other dogs. As Archie lay on a pile of blankets, the vet placed his stethoscope on Archie's chest then placed it in his lab coat pocket. He quietly took Betty, Bob and Dooley aside and whispered, "This may be it, I'm afraid. His breathing is labored. His heart isn't strong enough to maintain his functions. I'm sorry. You're welcome to stay here and say your goodbyes." The vet turned and left.

Betty and her six children surrounded the great wolfdog as they sat and stroked him. His brown eyes opened then closed. Bob put his head close to Archie's ear. "Remember all the good times we had, Archie. There'll never be another dog like you."

Dooley bent down, tears flowing down his cheeks. "Archie," he said haltingly, "You saved my life. I wouldn't be here if it weren't for you. Please don't go. Stay with us a little longer."

Patrick, Maureen, Lisa and Timmer looked at Betty as they stroked Archie gently. Betty rubbed their backs as they whimpered over the dying dog.

Betty petted Archie's head and drew close to his ear. "The first part of your life, I wanted nothing to do with you, I thought you were bad. Then I realized how important you were to all of us. Now it is time to go to sleep, Archie. You will always be with us." Archie licked her hand. His chest heaved one last time as he appeared to summon all his strength by raising his head to look at each of them as if to say an individual goodbye. And then he was gone, his large lifeless body being covered in tears that flowed down the cheeks of seven people as they sobbed and hugged him.

For several minutes, no one spoke. They just stared at Archie.

Rubbing tears from her eyes, Betty exhaled gently. "We were so lucky, kids. Most people go through life and never experience having an Archie touch them in so many good ways. We have our memories of him now. Hold onto them." The six children silently nodded, staring at the wolfdog, sniffling and wiping their faces with their sleeves.

Dr. Hosbach returned and took Betty aside. "I'm sorry for your loss. We have to decide now what to do with his body. We generally cremate animals and I can arrange for you to receive his ashes, if you want." Betty consulted with the kids.

"Let's take care of Archie ourselves, Mom," Dooley softly said. "It just doesn't seem right to burn his body." Turning to Dr. Hosbach, Dooley continued, "We can take him with us, right?"

"He's your dog, son. Do what you think is right."

They wrapped Archie in a large gray blanket. Bob and Dooley led the procession carrying Archie out of the clinic and they loaded him in the back of the car.

"We have to take Archie home," Bob said. The others nodded quietly.

"You're right, Bob," Betty gently said, placing her hand on his shoulder. "Archie deserves to rest where he spent the important moments of his life." They drove to the house to get a shovel. While Bob got that from the garage, Dooley went upstairs and put some things into a small bag.

Betty went inside, consulted her phone book and dialed a number. After three rings, a raspy man's voice said "hello."

"Art, it's Betty O'Neill. Sad news here. Archie just died. The kids and I want to bury him in Cazenovia. That spot on the edge of your land overlooking the lake, do you think we could lay him there?"

"Sorry to learn about Archie. Like a member of the family passing on. Be my honor to have him here."

"Thanks, Art. We'll be there in about an hour."

Everyone piled back into the car and they drove an hour up Route 20 to Cazenovia. During the ride, Dooley kept looking back at the blanket covering a still form. Maureen, Lisa and Timmer knelt on the back seat next to Dooley occasionally touching the blanket and looking at each other. Patrick and Bob just stared at the never ending white line in the center of the country road. Betty looked at the boys beside her and glanced behind her at the backs of the other four children whimpering and pawing the gray blanket.

Trying to break the morose silence, she spoke in a hushed tone, "Kids, let's talk about our favorite Archie memory." No one appeared in a mood to talk.

Pulling into town, they stopped at Smith's Market where Bob went in and returned a few minutes later. "Let's take Archie on one last trip around the paper route," Bob said.

"Yeah, good idea," Dooley said. "Archie would like that."

They started at Ryan's Funeral Home where the boys would go with Archie to collect the newspapers for their route. Dooley looked from the car into the familiar garage with the long wooden bench where Jack Ryan would load each paperboy's pile. "Bob, remember how excited Archie would get when we wrapped the papers with rubber bands. He used to put his paws up on the bench and watch every move we made. And then when we loaded them in those big baskets on our bikes, he would start prancing around barking. He couldn't wait to get that first paper in his mouth to deliver. Boy, he made our job easy."

Bob nodded. "You can say that again. I'm still amazed how smart he was. After he delivered to certain houses the first couple of times, we never had to remind him where to go. It took me a month to train Eddie McCauley when he took our route the two weeks we went away to Camp Eatonbrook."

They passed Aikman's Hardware and across the street the Theobald and Hole Drug Store. "Archie sure loved those places," Dooley said, pointing to the two stores. "Every day, two treats."

As they approached Cazenovia Lake, Patrick sat up. "I think if they had an Olympics for dogs, Archie would win a medal for swimming. He sure could go a long way out there." Everyone stared at the lake and shook their heads up and down.

They circled through town to the Troop 18 Scout Lodge. "Whenever I think of Thursday nights, I'll picture Archie going with us to our weekly meetings," Bob said. "I can't imagine any other dog liking camping and hiking as much as him."

They drove past the Cazenovia College tennis courts and Betty cleared her throat to make a comment. "Well, boys, I won't forget the phone call I got from Mrs. Eckel, the College President, asking me to check whether Archie was stealing their balls. Well, of course, he was."

Dooley sat up. "Yeah, Mom, it took Bob and me a long time to break him of that habit. Archie thought any tennis ball that flew over the hedges was his. I remember the first time I saw about seventy of those balls piled up behind the garage. It wasn't like he had enough. He just had to keep getting more."

"Well, I'm glad you boys trained him because that put me in an awkward position every time I went into her office to do substitute work."

As they entered the village green and passed St. James Church, they turned the corner and approached the school. "Archie sure spent a lot of time at that front door," Maureen said.

"Yeah, and he got a diploma for perfect attendance," Lisa said with certainty. "I bet there's no other dog will ever get one of those."

"I'll remember all those people standing and clapping when Mr. Schumard put that diploma in Archie's mouth," Bob said, staring at the lawn in front of the school. "There's just so many things Archie did that made him special."

Moments later, the battered station wagon pulled alongside their old house and stopped, engine idling. They all stared at the house silently for a minute where they had spent the vast majority of their days with Archie. Dooley looked up the Sullivan Street hill. "As long as I live, I will never forget that day. I remember it was late in the afternoon. Bob and I were in the yard playing catch. We looked up the hill and saw this animal limping as it came toward us. Then we realized, it was Archie. He came home to us from almost 20 miles. How? He wasn't even a year old."

"I think it was a miracle," Patrick said. "The angels were looking out for Archie. Just like they will be now." Everyone nodded.

They drove two blocks back to the lake where Dooley got out and laid on the end of the pier where the water was shallow and stuck his arm in, then walked back to the car. The others looked at him quizzically. "Just one more thing for Archie," he said. After a few minutes they pulled up to Art Evans' house, which stood on a hill overlooking the town and the lake.

Bob approached Art who was rocking on his front porch puffing on his corncob pipe. Art rose and shook Bob's hand and nodded to Betty as she and the others trudged to the house. "Mr. Evans, we brought Archie home. Can we bury him under that oak?"

"I'm sorry for your loss, Bob. Be my honor to have Archie rest here. It's good to see all of you, even under these sad circumstances. I think of Archie as the finest canine citizen Cazenovia ever had. In fact, we got a nice picture of him hanging in the scout lodge right over the fireplace. We tell all the new scouts about Archie. Got a picture of him in my office back at the hardware store, too. Every time I look at those pictures it brings a smile to my face."

"Thank you, Art," Betty said softly with a slight grimace.

"Anything I can do to help?"

"No, we can handle it," Bob said.

"Take all the time you need." Art settled back into his rocker and lit his pipe.

Bob and Dooley carried Archie the short distance from the car to the oak tree. Betty and the others trailed. Patrick carried the small bag Dooley had brought from home.

"What about this spot?" Bob asked. The others nodded approvingly. The late afternoon sun was setting over the edge of Cazenovia Lake. Bob and Dooley took turns digging the large hole. When they agreed it was deep enough, the two boys gently laid Archie at the bottom and climbed out.

"Patrick, can I have that bag now?" Dooley took it.

"What's that, Dooley?" Betty asked.

"While you were on the phone to Mr. Evans we decided to bring some things for Archie, stuff that will always remind him of the good times. Everybody thought of something to give him."

From the bag Dooley withdrew a tennis ball and handed it to Timmer who tossed it on the blanket as he said, "Here's something you can use in heaven, Archie, when you find somebody who wants to play catch."

Then Dooley removed an old football with the leather exterior almost completely chewed off, revealing the under layer of pigskin. He handed it to Maureen. "You always liked these balls the best, Archie. This one's really good and chewed."

Next, Dooley removed a Boy Scout insignia that read 'Troop 18' and handed it to Bob who dropped it in the grave. "Whenever I think of the scouts, I'll always remember you, Archie. All the other members of our troop will too. You made it a lot more fun for all of us."

Dooley brought out a small triangular banner, blue with yellow trim, with the words 'Cazenovia Central School'. He handed it to Lisa. As they watched it flutter on top of the blanket, Lisa smiled a little and then took the bag from Dooley for a moment. She withdrew an old shoe and added that to the grave. "Thanks, Archie, for showing up with my other shoe. I never got out of milk duty again. I hope they have a school in heaven where you can sit and greet everybody."

Dooley handed Patrick a copy of that day's Syracuse Herald Journal, wrapped in a rubber band. Patrick tossed it on top of the other items. "I don't think there's ever going to be another dog who delivers newspapers like you, Archie. If they have a paper route in heaven, I think God will have you do it."

Dooley took the paper bag from Smith's Market and removed a small package wrapped in wax paper. He handed it to Betty. "Well, Archie," she said as she unwrapped the paper to smile at a turkey drumstick, "I will always think of you every Thanksgiving. You had a fine feast one year and I was ready to give you away. I am so happy I didn't. You became a constant love in our lives and you will always be in our hearts."

Standing over the grave, Dooley reached into his pocket and pulled out a Boy Scout Lifesaving Merit Badge. "Archie, if it weren't for you, I would not be here today. I will remember you every day of my life. Even though I received this badge, you're the one who really earned it. Thank you for saving my life."

Dusk had arrived as the boys shoveled the last of the dirt over Archie's body. Tears dripped off faces on to the overturned soil.

"Let's say a prayer for Archie so the angels will speed him on his way," Betty said.

They recited a Hail Mary and blessed themselves saying in unison, "In the name of the Father, the Son and the Holy Ghost."

Dooley pulled a small, shiny rock from his pocket and placed it at one end of the grave.

"What's that for, Dooley?" Betty asked.

"Dad's not here today. But he'd be the saddest of all if he were. He and Archie had a special way of talking to each other. I thought maybe Dad had some magic power to talk to dogs. I don't know if he did. For sure, he understood Archie, maybe just reading his eyes. And Archie, he understood Dad even if Dad said nothing. Dad told me he talked to him a lot about Archie's responsibilities in our family. And Archie must have understood because look what he did.

"Anyway, Dad told me this story about a thing he did whenever he set somebody's gravestone. He said he always put a pebble from Cazenovia Lake on it. Something he heard the Onondaga Indians that lived here hundreds of years ago did when they buried one of their own. He said the rock connected the dead person with those burying him. This rock will always be with Archie and make him part of us. I think Dad would like that Archie had a stone. "

Everyone shook their heads in agreement. Betty put her arm around Dooley's shoulders and smiled at him.

Patrick looked up at his mother. "Archie will like it here, Mom. His spirit can go all the places he used to walk." While keeping one arm around Dooley's shoulders, Betty put her other arm around Patrick's shoulder as she kissed his forehead.

In the distance, a wolf howled.